MW01016498

Don't
Clone a
Snowflake

Rebecca Goudreault

 FriesenPress

Suite 300 - 990 Fort St
Victoria, BC, V8V 3K2
Canada

www.friesenpress.com

ISBN
978-1-5255-2275-8 (Hardcover)
978-1-5255-2276-5 (Paperback)
978-1-5255-2277-2 (eBook)

1. FAMILY & RELATIONSHIPS, CHILDREN WITH SPECIAL NEEDS

Distributed to the trade by The Ingram Book Company

And I Pray that you grasp how wide and how long
and how high and how deep is the Love of Christ
(Eph 3: 17–18 [New International Version Bible]).

RECENTLY SOMEONE ASKED ME THE question, "What is the 'heartbeat' of your book?" I thought it over, if there was only one answer to that question what would it be. A short time later I heard a sermon and whereby I felt the Lord answered the question. The pastor said he was in Mexico when he was watching a line-up of local people waiting for food. In the line-up he noticed a young mother holding her child who was probably about two years old. This child appeared somewhat sick, as his nose was runny and his eyes were teary. The pastor had compassion come over him, so he went over to the child and laid his hands on the child's forehead to pray. As he did he looked into the child's eyes and saw Jesus. The child looked back into the pastor's eyes and gave the pastor a big smile. The Lord spoke to the pastor and said, "When he smiled at you he saw me in your eyes."

Now when I heard that story, I smiled to myself as I knew that's how Joey and I communicated with each other. The "heartbeat" of this book was the love of Jesus, the center of Joey's story. That also explains the peace I experienced despite the circumstances. God's love reigned as I did my utmost to keep my mind on the Lord, who was and is my heavenly Father and Friend. I discovered you can not depend on feelings or anything else, only God is dependable.

The title "Don't Clone a Snowflake" is a message I hope to pass on, but the "heartbeat" is that Jesus' presence was ever-present, as close as Joey was. God's living Word became alive to me.

"Oh taste and see that the LORD is good; blessed is the man who trusts in Him!" (Psalm 34; 8)

This is a story about a snowflake named Joey who showed me God's love and I pray others will see the difference one little snowflake can make in a life. Joey made this song real to me:

"What a Difference You've Made in My Life"

What a difference you've made in my life.
You're my sunshine day and night.
What a change you have made in my heart.
You've replaced all the broken parts.
Love to me was just a word in a song that had been
way over used,
But you gave love new meaning
So I've joined in the singing,
That's why I want to spread the news,
What a difference you've made in my life.

(B.J Thomas)

Introduction

THIS IS JOEY'S STORY. JOEY stayed with us for only fifteen months, yet made enough of a difference to last a lifetime. I will always miss him but I could never wish him back. Joe is alive in heaven and he will become alive to others through his story, which he inspired me to write.

I do not believe I could fully express what Joey did for me. I can only share my experience. A door was opened when he was born. That door is still open. It did not close when he died because the love lives in me to stay.

My prayer is that the people, who read this story, may catch a glimpse of the pure love Joey passed onto others. I hope many will gain a greater appreciation for the very gift of life itself. Also, I pray Joe's story helps us to look upon the handicapped through the eyes of our Creator then go on to make a difference in many lives.

Firstly, I would like to thank God for creating Joey and giving me his precious life for a season. I would like to thank friends for their encouragement to write Joey's story and everyone who helped make Joey's life so much better. I know they were blessed for it. With all my heart, I want to thank the reader, for now my sorrows are not in vain. Joe had so much to give and he is still giving through this story.

Thank you Joey, for your gift of love!

Chapter 1
Preparation Time

ONE DAY WHILE SITTING IN church I heard the minister say these words: "You can believe that God has his eye on all children, all new babies and those yet unborn." I find it hard to describe how those words pricked my heart. I had this conviction that God had his eye on another baby for me. Throughout my life I had an impression that someday I would have a handicapped child and someday write a book. I believe the impression was Gods still small voice who knows all things. Psalms 139 verse 3 in the living bible **says; "You chart the path ahead of me, and tell me where to stop and rest. Every moment you know where I am"**. I never dreamed, however, that I would write a book about having a handicapped child.

I had little things happen, that I believe were preparing me for his birth. One of those little things I want to mention was a note. Someone I met at a woman's retreat while I was pregnant with Joseph gave me this little note. The note read:

"Dear Becky,

> We love you, and I give you this gift to last. You have brought me the chance to remember the excitement and hope of a new baby. This will be a very *special* child to all of us.

I feel the note was inspired, because that's just the way God works. It turns out; Joseph was a very special child to all of us. I felt like God was dropping hints long before Joey was born. Sometimes I would think about how excited Mary must have been to actually be told by an angel that she would give birth to the Savior of the world.

I had a spiritual, peaceful feeling whenever I would dream about my unborn child.

I sensed Joey would be special and perfect. I believed God was preparing me during my pregnancy. Never once did the though enter my mind that Joey would be handicapped. I was in for a surprise!

I learned life lessons during the season; only God knows everything. God never leaves you alone, God prepares you and never gives you more then you can handle, and most importantly *God is a good God*.

God was preparing me during my pregnancy for my perfect baby. I had faith for a perfect baby, but my faith didn't come with a blueprint. Challenges were to be part of my snowflake's life.

God's way of working things out was something I never thought about. God sees the whole picture while we can only see what is right in front of us. It is assuring to remember Proverbs 3:6: "In all thy ways acknowledge him and he shall direct thy paths."

God was with me in a defined way throughout Joey's life. I recall that lingering peaceful, feeling that stayed with me before Joseph's birth. I know it to be the peace that can only come from God. Maybe that's why I was so self-assured about everything. I had God's peace. John 14:27: "Peace I leave with you, my peace I give to you; not as the world gives do I give to you. Let not your heart be troubled, neither let it be afraid." Phil 4:6-7: "Be anxious for nothing, but in everything by prayer and supplication, with thanksgiving, let your requests be made known to God; and the peace of God, which surpasses all understanding, will guard your hearts and minds through Christ Jesus." That's just what happened to me.

Yes, the Lord's presence was ever so near. I couldn't believe anything could go wrong. This loving presence was confirming my belief that I would not only have a beautiful baby, but also a perfect baby.

A new baby comes with the excitement of picking a name. My desire was to pick just the perfect name for my perfect baby. I often remarked that I knew it was to be a boy. I just knew that I knew. One day as I was thinking about a baby's name I said, "What about the name Joseph?" In that moment, I was overwhelmed with the presence and joy of the Lord. It did not surprise me too much, as I was actually getting used to such experiences. The conviction was getting stronger that this was God's baby and He had a special plan for the baby's life. The name Joseph was finally chosen in the hospital the day before his birth. The Lord knew the baby's name all along, as He knows everything. Yet up to that day I wasn't sure. There were several other names that I had in my mind, but I decided Joseph would be a good name for him as Joseph was the youngest of brothers in my favorite bible story and my baby Joseph would be the youngest in his family.

I recall certain experiences when pregnant with Joey. Throughout my life I've had dreams that were impressed so strongly in my mind that I will never forget them. I had several significant dreams during my pregnancy with Joey. The day before I had one of these dreams, I recall a conversation with God. It went something like this: I was standing at the kitchen sink at the time washing dishes and I said, "Dear God, I can't understand this wonderful feeling of happiness

I have right now. It must be because of you. Anybody looking in from the outside probably thinks I should be miserable. I feel so fat and pregnant. I have a demanding toddler in diapers, little time to call my own, barely making it financially; and my husband and I have problems. How in the midst of these things can I still possess such a feeling of happiness? God, most of the time I feel trapped, chained to the house. Is there a special meaning to happiness, and what do I need to do to really understand it? If you could let me know God, I would really appreciate it; In the name of Jesus, Amen.

That night I had a dream about happiness, even though when I had finished praying that day I forgot about the prayer. Yet God remembered and faithfully answered in this dream that came to me in parables and I put it in my journal. In one of the parables in this dream I was surrounded by my church friends and we passed someone constantly working. It seemed that all this man was concerned about was working. We decided that someone should t tell him to take some time to enjoy life. This man said he would, and we all came away from the experience with this beautiful feeling of happiness. The thought entered my mind: that's real happiness, simply showing someone that there's more to life than just work. In the other parables of this dream all my friends helped each other whenever we had a need. I felt very rich to have these friends. In another scene in my dream I saw people working at jobs that they really enjoyed doing. In another, I enjoyed simply talking with someone I really loved. In each parable, I was left with the idea that happiness is so simple. It is just giving and sharing whatever we can, and in return we reap what is sown. By reaching out to others we can't help but be blessed abundantly. God will give us our reward.

In Galatians 6:2, "Bear one another's burdens, and so fulfill the law of Christ"; "And let us not grow weary while doing good, for in due season we shall reap if we do not lose heart" (Gal. 6:9); and "Therefore, as we have opportunity, let us do good to all, especially to those who are of the household of faith" (Gal. 6:10). Luke 6:38

is another scripture that supports the value of giving. It says: "Give and it will be given to you: good measure pressed down, shaken together, and running over will be put into your bosom. For with the same measure that you use, it will be measured back to you."

One of my favorite scriptures is Psalm 16:7-8: "I will bless the Lord who has given me counsel; my heart also instructs me in the night seasons. I have set the Lord always before me; because He is at my right hand I shall not be moved." I felt like God had given me a little nugget of wisdom in a dream. I learned that happiness is so simple, that it is people who make it complicated. Scriptures started to come alive and have meaning for me. My experiences have shown me that these scriptures do hold true. We must exercise them. For example, James 1:5 goes as follows: "If any of you lack wisdom let him ask of God, that gives to all men liberally, and up braideth not, and it shall be given to them." It goes on to say in James 1:6: "But let him ask in faith, nothing wavering, for he that wavered is like a wave of the sea driven with the wind and tossed." By practicing these biblical principles, one is always continuing to learn to trust in Jesus and without faith it is impossible to please Jesus. It is good to be reminded of the verse in Proverbs 16:16: "How much better it is to get skillful and Godly Wisdom than gold! (The Amplified Bible)

I have come to realize beyond a shadow of a doubt that things we cannot hold in our hands or see with the naked eye are what make life really worth living. Every situation in our lives can be learning experiences if we will allow it to be.

The preparation, birth, and life of Joseph were all eternal lessons about Gods love.

Since childhood, I was a dreamer. My first spiritual experience was in a dream, yet this one was more like a visitation than a dream. This particular dream happened about two months after I committed my life to Jesus when I was seventeen years old. I was making every effort I knew how to live for Jesus. At this time, I was praying for a real spiritual experience because I wanted to say I was born again and know without a doubt that Jesus was real. I was having a few problems at school, which caused me to pray earnestly this particular night. During the night, I remember feeling so awake yet asleep. I looked over at my bedroom window and had a vision of a beautiful golden cross appear. The cross passed out of sight, in its place appeared what was like a z of lighting; such a pure indescribable heavenly white. It quickly passed and then I felt the presence of the Lord. I sensed that the Lord was at the foot of my bed, but I was unable to look at Him. I became utterly overwhelmed and taken up into the most intense feeling of love. Immediately, I got out of my bed, onto bended knee, and was only able to utter, repeatedly, "Oh Jesus, how I love you." This was my first God encounter of ultimate love in a supernatural dream. I knew for myself that Jesus was as close as my breath.

My foundation and beliefs took me through the difficulties I had with my Down syndrome baby. My snowflake was a blessing with some challenges, yet I knew my Creator as a good God.

I had another answer to prayer before Joey's birth, another building block in my ever-growing faith in the Lord. This prayer had to do with my daughter Desiree's "baby blessing." We planned to have the blessing done on Mother's Day. Desiree was born in 1979, the Year of the Child. I wished for a daughter and Desiree was that wish fulfilled. Desiree's baby blessing was at church out of town so her grandparents could attend. Our most special friends in the world were supposed to come, too, but they informed us it would take a miracle for them to get time off work to travel. Well I told them (John and Lona Lowe) that if we don't believe in miracles, then who will? After the conversation, I said out loud, "I won't believe they won't be there unless I see it with my own eyes." Now when I look back, I see how powerful our words can be. While at the church waiting for the service of Desiree's baby blessing to begin, I suddenly heard a whisper: "If we don't believe in miracles then who will?" and as I turned around I was elated to see my special friends made it to the service. Thank you Jesus was all I could think. I had confirmation of a loving Jesus who cares and loves me, even in the small stuff. God just loves to shower blessings and favor on His children. Matthew 7:7-8 says, "Ask, and it will be given to you; seek, and you will find; knock, and it will be opened to you" and "For everyone who asks receives, and he who seeks finds, and to him who knocks it will be opened."

God hears our prayers and is concerned with what concerns us. I believe the best way to hear and learn from God is to read his love letters in the Bible. If God's word speaks to you from other sources, it will be confirmed from the Bible. God has spoken many times in dreams throughout history. For example, in Mathew 2:12: "Having being warned by God in a dream not to return to Herod, they departed for their own country by another way." Also, Mathew 1:19–20: "And her(promised) husband Joseph, being a upright man and not willing to expose her publicly and to shame and disgrace her, decided to repudiate and dismiss (divorce) her quietly and secretly. But as he was thinking this over behold and angel of the Lord appeared to him in a dream saying Joseph descendant of David, do not be afraid to take Mary (as) your wife, for that which she conceived is of (from, out of) the Holy Spirit."

A whole study could be done on the subject of dreams.

I only know what I experienced with my dreams. God-given dreams helped to prepare me for much in my life. I ignored and didn't understand several of my dreams concerning the birth and life of Joey, but I know now the Lord was preparing me for Joey.

One dream that happened went like this: I was sitting in a wheelchair in the hospital, talking on the phone to a doctor long-distance. In the dream, the doctor wanted permission to give my baby a colostomy. The next day I asked what a colostomy was, but no one I asked knew. I had certainly never heard of such a thing, so I brushed it off as a silly dream, yet that's exactly what happened. I found out quickly what a colostomy is when Joey was born, as he needed an emergency colostomy. I wished I would have listened to my dream.

Often, I heard myself speaking things out loud like, "I do not know why, but there is going to be something special about this baby. I cannot imagine what, but I hope it's nothing bad." God was trying to speak, but I had poor listening skills.

In the long run, we would all be better off if we just lived life a little less busy and had quiet times to hear God speak to us. We miss too much living life in the fast lane.

I knew my prayers were heard if I prayed sincerely. I have always said that we better be careful what we pray for because we just might get it. I can still remember some of those prayers I offered up to the Lord regarding Joey. I dedicated Joey to God as I was so thankful and blessed with two other special snowflakes. My prayer was, "Dear God, this is your child so whatever you decide is just fine with me."

When I was expecting my second baby (Desiree), I just decided I was going to have a girl. I told everyone I had put in my order upstairs before she was conceived. It seemed very simple to me. I was very specific with God about details. Well, no one told me I couldn't and she is exactly the answer to my prayer. I named her Desiree as the name means a wish for a daughter fulfilled.

The Bible says men ought to pray. Luke 18:1: "Then He spoke a parable to them that men always ought to pray and not lose heart." Matthew 17:20: "So He said to them, Because of the littleness of your faith (that is, your lack of firmly relying trust) For truly I say to you, if you have faith like a grain of mustard seed, you can say to this mountain, Move from here to yonder place, and it will move; and nothing will be impossible for you."

The bible says to pray and so I did. Joey was dedicated from my heart to the Lord before being born. "God is a good God" was my theme song and still continues to be so. My feelings about having a Down syndrome baby remain that *God is a good God.*

God wants us to be happier than we can imagine and enjoy what we have. Jesus made each of my children special and unique. Down syndrome just means unique individuals with similar characteristics, such as a slightly flat nose, slanted eyes and shorter in stature. Often the most noticeable characteristic is the slanted eyes. Some say the eyes are the mirror to the soul. I only know that in Joey's slightly slanted eyes, I saw the love of Jesus and his smile brought a smile to the faces of all those lives he touched.

Praise to the Lord for the power of prayer, our telephone line to heaven.

Yes, time has taught me how God honors our prayers, and how we need to honor Him as our Father. I often talk to God as my daddy, taking all my silly worries to Him. I requested that Joey would be a quiet, contented baby, as life was busy. The peace of God would come and I knew Joey would be a peaceful baby. Joey was just that.

One day, Darren, my oldest son, and I were talking about whether Joe would be a boy or girl. I asked Darren what he thought, girl or a boy. He replied, "It's going to be a boy." Darren at the age of eight, he knew.

Joey was an angel to us and the birth of an angel is quite an event. God had a plan, a special purpose for Joseph's life. Because of Joey's life, we were able to draw closer to our Heavenly father by learning to trust in him for all he had planned for Joey's life, and to have compassion for others with disabilities.

I could feel prayers from people. I am convinced Joey needed prayers in order live as long as he did. One friend suggested that I should have special prayers, as the Bible says, "by the laying on of the hands." James 5:14: "If any among you is sick. Let him call for the elders of the church, and let them pray over him, anointing him with oil in the name of the Lord and the prayer offered in faith will restore the one who is sick, and the Lord will raise him up, and if he has committed any sins they will be forgiven him."

Joseph had a lot of prayers!

I don't know where my faith in prayers began, because I can't ever remember not praying. Long before Joey came along I remember prayers being answered. Prayers are building blocks for ones faith.

One of those major building blocks for my faith was a prayer said on behalf of my dear sister Betty before she died. Betty was my first of several close loved ones that I lost too early. I was only twenty-four and she was thirty-four, leaving behind six young children.

One day Betty had to catch a bus alone to go to a hospital and was very nervous about this trip. Betty requested a special prayer from the family. Later, Betty told us how a lady helped her at every bus stop and had coffee with her. Betty remarked about how strange it seemed that the lady had seemed to read her mind and encourage her. Betty said the lady always appeared at the right place and the right time to help her. The lady told Betty that she shouldn't think of herself as some big sinner just because she smoked. That made me think "guardian angel." Betty was blessed because she remembered to ask for prayer.

From Mathew 18:20: "Where two or three are gathered together in my name, there I am in the midst of them." Yes, God's words hold true. That day for Betty was a testimony of God's love for her. Betty was a mom, a sister, and a friend rolled into one for me. My fondest memories of her were when she sang Christian songs to me when I was just a kid. The house rang with her voice, singing "Sweet Chariot" and "How Far is Heaven."

Once, Betty almost died in the hospital and she told me that she had looked over at the hospital curtains to see beautiful heavenly colors dancing across them and at same time heard the sound of angels singing, in such a beautiful way that she couldn't describe it, and a chariot appeared with a roman soldier and said to her, "Are you coming?" Betty said she answered, "No, I'm not ready." Betty said she looked away and she knew if she looked back she would have died. Betty lived another five years. I recall her last Christmas here on earth she told me she knew she would die soon. It happened six months later.

Betty and Joey have gone ahead of me, partying, while I tell their story. Both taught me that life is short but God is faithful and prayers reach heaven.

One of the first prayers on Joey's behalf was in the beginning of the pregnancy, during a church service. A wonderful friend prayed with much love, and tears. She asked our heavenly Father to breathe the breath of life into the little body with such earnestness. I was taken aback and always remembered that prayer. God not only answered my friend's prayer but told her what to pray for, as none of us knew Joey's little body had a large hole in his heart.

Faithful friends prayed for Joey before he was born and for me after he died. True friends when I needed them carried my backpack so my journey was not so heavy. Truly a blessing!

One the most beautiful joys was being a part of Joey's life. I know it was a miracle. I well remember the joy I had while carrying Joey for nine months. The wonderment of setting eyes on one's baby for the very first time is a miracle. How can anyone really explain the miracle of a new human life? I can't help but feel that babies attract us to them, as they just came from their real home in heaven. Joey always radiated heaven to me.

Up until the last month before Joey was born, everything seemed to be going along fine. The doctors did become concerned during the last month, because Joey stopped growing then. They also thought he was too small. I felt that there was no cause for alarm, as I was convinced my baby would be perfect. It turned out the doctors did have reason for concern but I felt great. All was well with my soul. I felt drawn closer to God through my babies!

I miss you, Joseph. I will always remember!

Chapter Two
Joey Is Born

JOSEPH JOHN PETRIE WAS BORN August 14, 8:21 a.m. 1981 at 5 lbs 0 ounces.

One of the first things given to me after Joey was born was a little poem that I loved. Even though a Christian, it was hard for me to understand what was going on with my perfect baby. I kept a verse from that poem, written by Edna Massionilla, which spoke to my heart and I personalized the poem. My short version of the poem follows below.

"Heaven's Very Special Child"

I did not realize right away
The leading role I was asked to play,
But with this child sent from above
Comes stronger faith and richer love,
And soon I knew the privilege given
In caring for my gift from Heaven

My precious charge, my snowflake
Is Heaven's Special Child.

I was reassured that God had a plan. I wanted all God had in store for me concerning Joey. I knew one thing from the beginning: Joey was a special child, yet a privilege to care for, as Joey gave me more love than one could ever give back.

The time for baby Joey to be born was drawing nearer and the doctor hospitalized me early. I needed rest due to my high blood pressure and I needed to have some test done.

Two weeks before the original due date, Joey arrived by caesarean birth. The tests helped the doctors make the decision to take Joey early. They said the baby would have a better chance in the outside world than inside me. I doubt the doctors knew how right their decision was. The doctors picked the thirteenth to perform C-section. I refused, saying, "Make it the fourteenth." I was nervous because my deaf brother was born on the thirteenth and I had some crazy idea that if anything was wrong, that's what I would blame it on. I am no longer superstitious. I just felt better about it, so the doctors kept me happy and the fourteenth was to be Joseph's birthday.

God sees all the details and is in everything. The scriptures confirm how God misses nothing. Job chapter 28 verse 24; says, "For He views to the ends of the earth and sees everything under the heavens." And Matthew chapter 10 verse 30; "And even the very hairs of your head are all numbered" (New International Version). I knew God was with me in every hospital room and everywhere.

Late in the morning on a hot summer day I saw Joey for the first time from my hospital bed. Having a caesarean section, I couldn't see Joey the minute he was born. The last thing I remember before Joey was born was the needle and feeling of someone starting to cut my abdomen. I looked at the clock, 8:00 am. I quickly drifted off, imagining that someone must be scratching my stomach. Two hours later I regained consciousness in the recovery room. My first thoughts went to my baby. I was so anxious to hear about him, yet very drowsy. Half-unconscious, I said to my nurse, "What did I have?" "A boy," she replied. Automatically I silently thought, oh, yes, of course, I knew it would be. Then quickly I asked, "Is he healthy?" Nobody answered. I spoke louder: "Is he healthy!" She answered with, "What did you say?" For the third time, I asked, "Is he healthy?" After a long pause, she said, "I don't know, you'll have to ask them down at the nursery." Despite being drowsy, I was immediately suspicious. It struck me very strange that she did not know. "She should know," I thought.

I now realize it was not her place to tell me about Joey's condition.

Back to recovery room, this nurse inquired if I was ready to go and see my baby. I was bursting with desire to see my new baby, like Christmas morning. Through this emotional experience, I did have a lot of physical pain, more than I've ever had before or since. I really had no pain from the surgery. My back was just excruciatingly painful from the way I was laying during surgery. I was spared pain from the C-section, which was a relief because I know it would have been intolerable to have both.

All the physical pain I had wouldn't come close to the emotional pain I was about to feel at the nursery. My heart broke.

So there I was, lying in the hospital bed, looking through the nursery window. "Where is he?" I asked my nurse. "Right there," she pointed. I looked over to where she pointed. I couldn't help but notice how doctor seemed to be fussing over Joey instead of just bringing him to me. At that moment I burst into tears, even before I was aware of anything concerning Joey. Somehow in the spirit or senses, I knew something happened to my baby.

My eyes met Joey's dads as he slowly came out of the nursery to my bedside with a strange look on his face. Joey's dad uttered not a word; the nurse carried Joey over to me. We discussed how much Joey reminded us of my dad. We talked about Joey's chubby little cheeks and little eyes. I insisted Joey's dad hold him so as I could have a real good look, to have my motherly inspection time. My baby was beautiful. Joey was my angel!

My first thoughts of Joey left as fast as they had come once the doctor started talking. I was confused. The conversation started with Joey's dad who said, "There are a few problems." I felt my heart jump and replied, "Nothing that can't be fixed, I'm sure." I was taken aback when his answer was, "No, can't be fixed." The worst filled my mind as I thought, Oh not death. I quickly looked at him square in the eye, remarking, "This is no time to be funny." The doctor then joined in and started to explain Joey's problems. One problem led to another.

The Doctor said Joey had no anus opening and would require emergency surgery for a colostomy. The surgery would entail making and opening on my baby's stomach to lift some intestine to the surface, which was called a stoma, so Joey would then be able to pass stool into a plastic bag (which are called colostomy bags). This sounded completely foreign to me. Then it got worse. She continued on, saying that Joey had a serious heart problem and needed more tests, but I should be prepared as it could also require immediate surgery.

I thought I was dreaming. Could all this be going on with the baby cradled so close in my arms? Then she told me all these problems were related to a condition known as Down syndrome. My nurse said she assisted my doctor in the operating room and detected immediately that my baby had Down syndrome. For a brief moment, there was silence. I choked on the words, "That isn't retarded, is it?" In a gentle voice, as tears came to her eyes, she answered, "Yes, it is."

What has gone wrong? Maybe I'm still in the recovery room having a bad dream. I was supposed to have a perfect baby. I was shocked. I felt my Joey touching my side, so helplessly. I am awake.

I'm not dreaming. My baby is beside me and he is mine. This was reality.

In shock, I had so many mixed emotions. For a moment I thought, I better not let myself love Joey, what if I lost him? Then I thought maybe it was wrong to love a baby who was different, as the doctor said something about making decisions. What on earth could she be talking about? I was trying to feel what was right, yet felt all the wrong things. I realized that I loved my baby instantly, only I didn't know how to react to what was happening. The emotional roller coaster was perfectly normal. If I could relive that conversation with the doctor I would say, "Don't clone a *snowflake.*"

God did help prepare me for the event of Joey's birth. Time and time again, I knew in my heart that Joey was a gift from God and would make such a wonderful difference in my life.

God made the difference possible! There really was nowhere to go but to the Lord. He was my source of strength and comfort.

Negative thoughts crept in occasionally. I did manufacture my own hell for awhile, but it did not take away from the love I felt for my baby or my faith. God was very near. I was mother bear where Joey was concerned. I know now we should not feel bad for our feelings. We cannot help but react to things that this world bestows upon us. We often come out stronger and wiser for the experience, but when in the middle of hard times we often are too caught up to see clearly and respond correctly. Fear of the unknown gripped occasionally. No matter what, I had to face the problems and place all my trust in God. It definitely was a learning experience. Through the pain came growth. Joey played a major role in the growth of my spiritual walk.

God held my hand. Joey was blessed on his day of birth. I recall thinking, "We won't forget this day either. Joey was blessed on his birthday and his sister Desiree was blessed on Mother's Day. In the bible Jesus took the children upon his knee and blessed them and it was dedication unto the Lord. Considering the circumstances, no time was wasted in blessing baby Joey, as we wanted all of God's best for Joey from the beginning. The prayer of blessing requested strength and miracles for parents, and Joey Joseph received the prayer of blessing on his birthday, August 14th, just prior to his jet ride to a children's hospital. I saw small and big blessings in Joey's short life span. My friend Lona encouraged me many times, saying how Joey would play a major role in my spiritual growth. Little did I know how that was the gospel truth. Joey did make such a difference. And thanks to God's many other challenges in life, I am still growing.

Everything I heard about Down syndrome came back to me that morning of Joey's birth. I knew I had to find out all there was to know about this condition. I needed to know how other parents of these children dealt with it and how their lives were affected by it. I wondered about what kind of reactions I would get from other people. I did receive a variety of reactions. I knew I would stand firm till the end and God had been preparing me for such a time as this.

I went back to the little I did know about Down syndrome. I recalled what I learned in grade seven health classes. I remembered how they taught it was a chromosome defect that could happen to anyone. I remember how it affected me way back at that time, as I was only the age of twelve. I can remember thinking to myself, "This is enough to scare one out of ever having babies; it could even happen to me." I grew up with a fear of people with a mental handicap. Just the word retarded scared me. It was because it was something different to me, unknown, and fear of something I really had no experience about. Many of us are influenced by others and believe that such a thing is terrible. I am thankful now that people are becoming more educated concerning the welfare of people with Down syndrome. It was a lot to accept at the time, but I knew Joey really was God's child.

My soul was filled with love for Joey and my initial reaction was normal. Joey was perfect. I even entertained the idea that maybe I committed some big sin and Joey's problem was my punishment, or maybe I wasn't a good enough Christian. Thankfully, I had other experiences to draw from, which helped. My sister took me on a tour through a home for mentally handicapped people. I told my sister I was really quite scared around these "kinds" of people. She said there really was nothing to fear, as they were just people. I'm glad I went. The little incidents of that day really left an impact on me. While walking from one building to another, we passed a young man who I could tell immediately had Down's syndrome. He was smiling genuinely as he said, "Hi, Tillie." "Hi," Tillie replied. "How are you?" he asked. "Fine," Tillie answered. "Nice day today, eh Tillie," he remarked. "Yes," she said back. "See you tomorrow," he added as he continued on his walk. I remember thinking to myself, "I thought this was a place for crazy people, why he's more pleasant than the average guy on the outside, and a happy, friendly fellow. Who would put him in a place like this?" That experience stayed with me.

My Joseph would know a loving home life. He would have grown to be the best he could have been. We all loved him so. Joey was a planned baby; three children were what we wanted. Joey was a sheer joy. The memories baby Joey left behind brought so much sunshine to my soul.

From day one I was on a mission to show the world what a joy Joey really was.

Nonetheless, it was a lot to accept, having a Downs baby with a large hole in the center of his heart and no anus opening. The Lord was ever so near and I came to clearly see how God was working things out for the best. It was like God was always providing a comforter so I wouldn't hurt so badly. Sometimes trusting God for His will was accepting. I might not receive just what I thought I wanted or needed. It's kind of like "The Father knows best." I know God provided for my needs, teaching me faith through all the little details He took care of in my life.

The Bible teaches us in Romans 8:28: "And we know that to them that love God all things work together for good, [even] to them that are called according to [his] purpose."

Yes, the difference Joseph made started the very first day. It seemed to be almost impossible for so much to happen in just one day. We make our plans but we never know what the day will bring.

Our first visit was cut short, as they whisked Joey back to the incubator and me down to my hospital room. That feeling of separation took over. It felt terrible. One thing I dreaded was being separated from my newborn. I felt we needed each other more than ever.

I was embarking on roller coaster ride of discovery.

There are a lot of changes to be made concerning the birth of any baby, so it's normal to have a difficult time when a child is born needing special medical attention.

I always turned to God and I knew there was an answer or a reason. I would never give up regarding my baby and God. The worst of my fears and tears lasted only about a month; I had to go through these feelings just like anyone else, despite my faith in God.

I was left with a strong yearning just to hold any baby when I was first separated from my newborn. My heart would just leap whenever I heard the babies crying across the hall. To this day, I love the sound of a baby crying.

As soon as I was able to get out of bed, I went over to see the other babies. I found it comforting to hold any baby. It helped knowing the Joey was in the best care possible without my presence. I had only one picture to hang on to and that was seeing my baby in the incubator before they whisked him off to the Children's Hospital and holding him in my arms with the ambulance attendant at my side. Joey was hooked up to all those monitors for the first time, and yet appeared so perfect to me. My heart cried out,

"How could anything be wrong, how could I be so wrong?" I took his little hand in mine, nervously noticing how his little heart was pounding so. I spoke out loud, not caring who might hear, just as long as my baby did. I said, "It's okay Joey, somehow we're going to make it." Deep in my soul I knew there just had to be a way. This was my baby and he just had to make it. I then started to cling to the thought that the Lord would simply grant us a miracle and would show everyone how perfect Joey was. I thought it's just a matter of sitting back and watching the miracles all come pouring down from heaven. And I wasn't so wrong about God, as He did provide many miracles. I knew it to be true that it was a miracle Joey was born alive and that he even lived at all. I have no doubt at all about that now. Things didn't work out the way I had them planned, but God's plan is always the best. One particular time, my pastor's wife was directed by God to send these ministers to us to pray that Joey would live. God sends prayers our way even when we are not aware we need them. The fact that they came showed me once again how God was concerned how important and powerful prayers really are. I really can't remember a prayer ever being longer on our behalf than that one. In that prayer, it was mentioned how I was to remember that Joey was really God's child, only for me to borrow. I couldn't understand the significance of the statement until later, when Joey was born and it took on such meaning as to why should I be worrying when Joey was really God's child. Surely He takes care of his own.

Not long after Joey's birth, my friend shared a story she heard about another parent who had a Down syndrome baby girl. Apparently, the father of the baby was very angry when it was discovered that his baby had this condition and he left the maternity ward and sped away in his car. He finally pulled the car over and yelled out to God saying, "Why did you do this to me." God answered, "You have been blessed." That was a real statement that I clung to. God was, I knew, in the blessing business.

I am able to look back and really recognize how God was ever so near; always working on the plan he had for Joey's life and mine. I knew full well that God was more concerned with every detail than I could imagine.

It was Joey's first day in this world and he got a jet ride to the hospital, all in a twenty-four-hour period. I'm sure Jesus held him in his arms through it all.

It was only one week later when Joey had his second plane ride, home to Kamloops. Joey still had to stay in the hospital for another month, but at least I was able to see him every day for as long as I wanted, which really helped me bond with Joey. A lot of rubble in my mind started to clear up, as it was so natural to love my baby. The nurses and doctors couldn't have been kinder and more understanding.

It was a process to accept some things. The first thing that took all my time was learning about a colostomy. I will never forget how I felt the first time I set eyes on it. I stood in awe as I watched the nurse change my baby's colostomy bag. The stitches were still there and to me it looked terrible. I thought I was going to faint but the nurses caught it and sat me in a chair. A piece of Joey's intestine was brought to the surface of his stomach, which is called a stoma in medical terms.

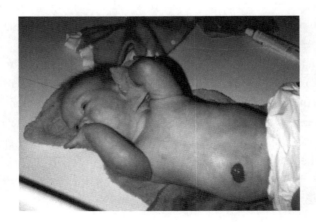

To me it was shocking, yet the nurses kept remarking how good it looked. That relaxed me some. Also, the specialist from Vancouver hospital had said that Joey was able to pass stool immediately when in most cases it took a couple of days and they remarked on how quickly it seemed to heal. Joey had no problems with it. It was obvious God was pouring in blessings. The colostomy was working so well for Joey. I also knew God was sending us the best of doctors, which was a blessing that wouldn't go unnoticed at such time. We know sometimes God chooses to work through doctors. My faith and respect increased in doctors because of my experiences.

I took over the nurse's job in order to take Joey home. I first had to learn this unappealing job of taking care of the colostomy. In the beginning, I believed I'd never be able to learn. I thought I wasn't smart enough for that but experience taught me well. It took some time to learn but once I did I knew it well. I even had to teach a nurse how to do it. It's definitely true to me that things we have to work harder at mean more than things that just come our way easily. I shed a lot of tears over that colostomy bag. What was normal was different. I learned a quick lesson through it all never again take anything for granted. So many others live with so much less. Daily existence is all some people will ever have. I learned what that attitude of gratitude is really all about, and sometimes life is joy with sorrow and often we grow the most during the hardest times of our lives. Lots can happen in one month's stay at a hospital.

I recall the longest day in the hospital before I was allowed to bring Joey home. The doctors did a heart cauterization test. The doctors had to put Joey to sleep for the test, as it was similar to surgery. I asked about the intravenous and nurse assured me that it would be removed before he returned to his hospital room. I watched as Joey received his first intravenous. It was inserted in the top of Joey's head, which caused a swelling that was supposed to go into the vein. I felt it, if that's possible. My apprehension was visible and nurse assured me it would be all right, as it was standard procedure. The intravenous had to be removed and a new one inserted. I wondered when this would ever end. I think the attending nurse took note of my anxiousness and decided to wait till down in surgery room before doing another intravenous. I really couldn't relish more of the same, even though I knew Joey would not escape more of the same.

Soon Joey was swept away for the big test. The time dragged and finally Joey returned to my side. I believed Joey would be fine and needed just some rest, but instead along came more intravenous tubes hanging off him. How could such a normal procedure, as the nurse had said, be so hard on my nerves? The tears welled up in my eyes and I was met with a sarcastic nurse, who bluntly remarked, "What's the matter?" To the nurse this was routine but it was gigantic to me, as just prior to leaving for surgery another nurse said Joey would have no intravenous when he returned. I was surprised to see otherwise. This nurse said it all was precautionary and the intravenous would soon be removed. I wished they all go together with the information. Just a job, I guess, for some nurses but my baby to me. That was a long day and an awakening to what lay ahead.

Joey's first month at hospital seemed to drag. I wanted Joey home. My good friend gave me a beautiful baby shower to cheer me up. I received so many nice things for my new baby, beautiful clothes and blankets. They made a money tree, which was enough to provide everything I needed for my beautiful baby, which encouraged me. I had all the best for Joey. It was as if God did the shopping himself. Every new mom needs something like a baby shower to celebrate the birth of a new baby, and I think maybe more so when the baby is one of special needs. Moral support is so important when a new mom has so much to deal with.

I learned more than just how to look after a colostomy that first month. I was exposed to other parents of sick children. I saw the dedication of moms for their sick children. They would just sit and talk so patiently to the child, comforting their children the best they knew how. The parents would also comfort the children nearby who were not their own. I picked up a certain bond between the parents of sick children who were strangers. I was able to listen and pray about all the things on my mind. We moms had very real obstacles to overcome. I struggled to nurse my baby. I felt that it might be hopeless, but the Lord's spirit would fill my soul and I was encouraged to not give up. The physiotherapist showed me some exercises to help strengthen the muscles around Joey's mouth, which I did faithfully, hoping so much it would help. God taught me to give everything to him and all I needed was to keep doing my best and let him do the rest. I had to draw on my faith to God. He was and is in the driver seat, I had to depend on that. Others tried often to sway my faith, saying things like, "How can you believe in something you cannot hold in hands or even see?" I knew better. No one can see the wind, yet everyone knows when it's blowing. Everyone believes in time, yet we can't hold that in our hands. All I have to do is look at the world and its beauty to see God and the work His hands have made. God hung the stars in order. How could all the Christians in the world be wrong? I can't see how anything would make any sense without a God. God created man, you and my Down baby. My faith carried me through and my love for Joseph overshadowed the fears in my heart.

I remember all the kind friends who God provided through the tough emotional times. While Joey was still in the hospital the first time around, I heard a little story that night from a friend. It went something like this: There was a little boy that wanted so badly to play in this orchestra, so he practiced and practiced until he could play his instrument, the flute. It came time for the orchestra to perform. The music began and the song went on and on until there was a pause. And it was the little boy's turn and he played—just one note on his flute. But the song couldn't have been played without that one part he had to do. Our friend went on to compare this story with Joey's life. How we don't know Joey's part. But to know it would be important and that it's God's work and the plan of our Savior. The more I learned, the more I realized how little I really knew.

Joey's life had purpose, wonder, and joy; just like one little note in one little song. Joey was a happy baby!

Don't clone a snowflake.

One other friend visited Joey in the first week of his life in the hospital. He related it to me, saying the visit deeply touched him. And when he was alone with Joey, he reached his hands into his incubator and laid his hands on him while he prayed. And after the prayer, he left the room, walked out of the hospital to the grounds, and noticed how beautiful the flowers were and what a bright sunny day it was. As he admired the beauty, God spoke to him and said, "Joey shall live to see all this." I felt so joyful when I heard this. I realize God granted Joey and me time. Joey lived through the following summer and we took walks outdoors on those very grounds.

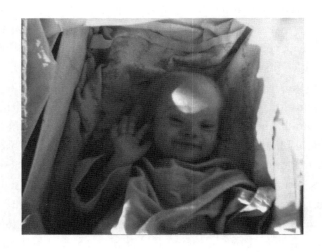

God only knows my gratitude for that experience and for praying friends.

Here is an insightful article from the book "Dawn without Darkness"

> Prayer touches our lives as we begin to do things we could not have done unless we had prayed. We begin to believe, we seek forgiveness, and we love those who otherwise would have been unlovable to us. Prayer is not a pious addition to things. It is a force allowing things to happen which could not have occurred without prayer. Even Jesus prayed before He went to the cross. He first prayed in Gethsemane.

(Anthony T. Padovano)

I was full of questions like, what was God's plan? What was this thing called faith? And how does one practice it? Thank God. He was and is my heavenly teacher. I decided that I had to trust the Lord more than ever. He is the Creator and had the whole world in His hands. I had to believe He was overshadowing all my steps. I certainly didn't have to understand everything; I just had to do my best to live by faith. As the bible says in Habakkuk 2:4, "the just shall live by faith." I learned a lot with the bible as my manual. I learned that we cannot just say we know God, but we must believe He works in our lives and not doubt that all things happen in His timing. By practicing faith, we in turn outwardly prove our trust in God. From Jeremiah 17:7: "Blessed is the man who trusts in the Lord And whose hope is in the Lord."

I discovered how much God speaks about love in the bible. How we should love one another as we love ourselves. How there is no greater love as a man who would lay down his life for a friend. I discovered I could never learn enough about love. Yet not once was

I taught this in school when I was growing up. I had to go to God to learn the greatest lesson in life. To know that real love comes from God. Only through Him can we truly love all people. God is love. It is the basis of all human needs. I know there is no such a thing as too much love. Experiencing love in its fullness gives life new meaning. I believe life should always be changing in order to keep growing and fulfilling all desires of a full and free happy life. An attitude of gratitude for the love of God keeps me on the right path. I understand better with a growing knowledge of the greatness of the word love. I believe God is love and is the greatest love relationship one can ever experience but yet not describe fully, only that when given away more comes back. Just like Joey's and my theme song says, "You give love new meaning."(B.J Thomas)

Chapter 3
Joseph Comes Home

JOEY'S INTRODUCTION TO THIS WORLD brought him *separation* from his mom, two *hospital* visits, one emergency surgery, and two jet rides. Not what I had expected. Once Joe was finally home, I was so thankful to have my baby home where he belonged. Along with the joy of Joseph's homecoming came the new vocabulary that I never used before. Words like *Down syndrome, heart problem, colostomy*, and *poor muscle tone* were suddenly everyday words. I was only twenty-eight with two young children also needing my attention. I needed God and faith and hope.

Major hurdles were overcome in time, along with gratitude that my baby had lived. Joey's homecoming was very special.

I dealt with anxiety, as now I had a special needs baby whose care was totally up to me and there was no nurse in the house, like at the hospital, who I could ask for help every time I felt unsure about something. I reminded myself that the doctors would not let me take Joey home in the first place if it was not going to be okay. Still, the homecoming brought some fretting due to the physical health conditions. I had a baby with a hole in the middle of his heart that was size of a quarter. That was a fact. It was difficult to get used to the sight of Joey's chest, as it looked like the heart was about to jump out of his chest at any given minute. Joey's heart was always racing, even with the medicine the doctors prescribed for it. Whatever happened to just Tylenol for fevers? Now it meant heart medicine. This was not my idea of fun. Nonetheless, we were not forgotten as we had a health nurse who came regularly. I was so thankful, as I still had a toddler and work never ended. At night, my thoughts would drift over into worries and uncertainties about my new baby's future. It was all still so new and I needed God's comfort and assurance. What I thought I needed was time. How I wish I knew then how little time I would have.

In the beginning of life at home with Joey, I never realized what a blessing the health professionals would be. The therapy for my special needs baby started early on. Joey's experience with health professionals continued his whole life. It began with enrolling in the infant development program and physiotherapy. I was eager to do the work to learn to help with Joey. The first exercise was eye tracking and it didn't take me long to see how the little exercises would end up making a big difference, although I see where I was also overprotective and believed the therapist would push my baby too far. I know this was due to Joey's little heart with the big hole. My feelings, I'm sure, were perfectly normal and as time passed so did my fears and my trust in the therapy increased. I had to over- come fears if I wanted to give my baby a fighting chance to have all life could give him. My hope was to have Joey grow up and have a whole healthy and full life.

I would pray the Serenity prayer: "God help me to accept the things I cannot change the courage to change the things I can, and the wisdom to know the difference." Praying consistently became a habit, over every little thing. It was a habit that took me through many challenges.

Breastfeeding turned out to be a lot of work. Downs baby have poor muscle tone—what should have been natural was more difficult. I was determined to do my best and ended up with many sleepless nights. One night I prayed that God would wake me up at two a.m. That night I awoke to a gentle, invisible hand on my check, pushing my head to one side. I looked at the clock which read 2:00 A.M. I remember feeling so tired so silently prayed for five more minutes. I instantly fell back to sleep and awoke at 2:05 A.M. to another gentle but firmer touch on my check, enough to cause me to jump immediately out of bed while at the same time making my apologies God. This was a beginning of many answers to prayer to help me mother my new baby. My daughter was a preemie and God brought good out of that experience and I came to know how much God cares about what concerns me.

I had to learn the real meaning of perseverance when it came to nursing Joey. After two months of trials, Joey still preferred the bottle. I was beginning to doubt that Joey would ever breastfeed and some discouragement set in. I was determined to do all I could to give Joey a good start in life. From my studies I was informed that breastfeeding helps prevent post-partum depression, protects one from certain chronic diseases, and causes estrogen levels to drop which helps guard against osteoporosis, diabetes, and hormone-related cancers (ovarian and breast). Also, it burns about five hundred calories a day assisting with new moms who have gained weight from pregnancy. Best of all it assists in mom-and-baby bonding. If nursing a baby did all that, I was going to preserve. It was work. I believed God would help Joey to have the nursing experience as God designed it in the first place but the day came that I felt I could not handle the work anymore. I had done my best. I had gone to classes and done my research. This was a real issue for me.

The day had come when I told myself I would make one last phone call before deciding to give up breastfeeding. I prayed first and the phone call led to an introduction to a lady named Norma who was to play an important part in our lives. I had a breakthrough. Norma was a professional nurse and a mom who had a Down syndrome boy who she nursed as a baby. She gave me excellent advice, which was to completely throw away the bottle and only nurse Joey for the weekend. She said Joey's confusion of what to drink would cease and Joey would become hungry enough to do the work of breastfeeding. Norma also stated that due to the low muscle tone in Down syndrome children it is more work but they can learn. I was skeptical but Norma reassured me Joey would not starve in only a couple of days. It all made perfect sense so with fresh hope I followed her advice. I first enlisted God by asking friends to pray for this need specifically. God heard my request and rewarded all my efforts. I can say I learned through this experience that God was there all along. God lined up help. The prayer request was specific in that God would quicken Joey's ability to nurse in accordance with God's will. That was all a short simple to the point prayer. I acted on my new friend's advice and tossed out the bottle. I waited on God and Joey, as it was no longer my problem. To my astonishment Joey nursed on the very first try. I cannot express the joy of success in what should have been natural. The perseverance paid off. It was quite a learning experience in not giving up. It may be a small accomplishment for some moms, but was another little miracle for this mom.

It was funny how Joey continued to nurse for almost four hours afterwards, except for burps and brief naps. Joey even nursed while napping. I was so happy that I probably would have let him continue all night. It was as if Joey was saying, "Oh now I get it!" I sensed such a peace and happiness. I thought to myself, I knew it would take Jesus to teach Joey this challenge. We landed the right teacher. I knew Jesus was in it all along but I had some learning to do along the way and it was so worth it. It meant the end to bottles, probably a healthier baby, and a happier mom. The work lessened.

God was not only my helper but my friend and my concerns concerned Him. Through the challenges I grew a gift of appreciation. I loved nursing more so because of all the work I did to achieve it. I will always look back on this as a great blessing. Things once insignificant suddenly take on meaning.

Joey was the sunshine of our family's life. I reflect on the blessings and miracles in awe.

Time passed too quickly.

All successes start with a single step. I am glad I have learned more perseverance through experience. I would like to make a note that some circumstances make it impossible to nurse one's baby and to remember there are other ways to ensure there's bonding and nutrition. No mom should feel guilty if they cannot nurse their baby. Love is the key ingredient to keeping them healthy and close and all moms can do that.

There's a little different version on this by William Shakespeare who said, "How poor are they that have not patience! What wound did ever heal but by degrees?"

Life at home had challenges to overcome, both physical and emotional. I don't know which is more difficult or if one can even compare.

The good thing is help was never far off. I was encouraged whenever I heard about other mothers who had similar challenges. I was never one to read the newspaper, but one day I did and an article caught my eye.(Abigail Van Buren)(Kamloops Newspaper, September 3 rd; 1981) .The column was by a mother who was saying just what I was feeling and it lifted my spirits. I have kept it to insert in this book, as I believe it may help other mothers, too.

Dear Abby,

This letter has taken me two and half years to write. It is in response to someone who asked if she should acknowledge a friend who had a baby diagnosed with Down syndrome.

Thank you for saying yes. The mother of such a child needs all the support and cheering up she can get.

I read that column the day I came home from the hospital with little Jimmy, my newborn Down syndrome baby. But there is so much more that [people need to know and as one who has had that experience, may I say it.

Please keep in mind that what happened to Jimmy was tragic but the child himself is not a tragedy and neither is his birth. He is such a loving member of our family as are our other children, so do send a card, a note or a little gift to acknowledge his birth.

Here are a few suggestions that will help you feel more comfortable when talking to parents of Down syndrome baby.

Please don't ask if insanity runs in the family. Down syndrome is a chromosome defect and is rarely hereditary. Furthermore, a Downs child is slow, which is vastly different from insane. It hurts moms to have people look upon one's child with pity.

Do not hesitate to ask how he is getting along. Some people avoid mentioning it as though he had died, because they think the situation is too horrible to even mention.

When the child seems to be progressing, please don't say he seems normal and maybe won't be retarded after all. New parents need to face up to the facts regarding their special child before they themselves can accept him.

By denying his limitations, you encourage false hopes and convey the message that you don't really accept or love him.

About one third of all Down syndrome children are born with heart defects. Our Jimmy required open-heart surgery. He survived the operation and is much improved. We thank God for that, so don't say it might have been a blessing if he had died. And don't be surprised that they would bother to operate on such a child. Please believe the parents when they say that their special child is a worthwhile little person and they are actually glad to have him. While Down syndrome is nothing to wish for, it can be accepted and is not nearly as catastrophic as it seems the first few weeks.

In the beginning the parents need to talk about their feelings. Don't argue. Listen. Let them weep- weep with them. When they can finally smile about their baby, you smile too.

Don't refer to the child as "that poor little thing." It hurts to think they wish he had never been born. He's not repulsive in the least and I can honestly say that much good has already come from our little treasure.

Our other children (eldest is 9) have learned understanding and compassion because of their little brother. We told them the truth immediately and they have loved him from the day they first saw him.

I cannot imagine life without Jimmy. HE IS THE SUNSHINE OF OUR LIVES. People often don't mean to be insensitive or cruel -they just don't know how to handle the birth of an exceptional child.

I know this is a long column, but I believe it will be a tremendous service to many.

Signed: Jimmy's Mother.

That's the ending of the column. It brought many a tear to my eye when read as a new mom in the same situation. I needed to cry at times, as I think the tears brought healing and much of the words Jimmy's mother said felt like my own. One can only truly relate when they have walked in the same shoes. The above column was printed many years ago and things have progressed in society as far as accepting and understanding of special need individuals. Unfortunately, there are many still in society who look down upon those individual with special needs. They call them the unfortunate ones. I prefer to call the uneducated society the unfortunate ones because of their lack of understanding. I have heard negative comments that are not even worth repeating about Down syndrome and handicapped individuals. I could not believe the lack of understanding and fears that are in pockets of society concerning special needs individuals.

When I first arrived home, I would save letters, poems, and anything in regards to Downs's information. I had my mind set to treat my handicapped baby perfectly normal, as my belief system told me Joey was perfect. I bought birth announcement cards. My mind would tell me, "Remember, Joey is handicapped" but my heart said, "He is perfect." I bought the nicest birth announcement cards I could find. The little cards said, "We have a baby boy and we are filled with joy." Despite all the hurdles and challenges I can honestly say I was filled with joy; the kind of joy that I suppose can only come from the Lord. As the Bible says, the joy of the Lord is my strength and so it was. I realized that some folks would not believe that we could really feel joy over the birth of a Down baby but I sure had it deep inside where it counted. And as Jimmy's mother wrote, it was very important to me to announce his arrival the same as I did with my previous two children. No one but the good Lord will ever know just how much a simple baby shower did for my well-being. Joey had the best of everything for a new baby, just as he deserved. And even though Joey's stay with me was far too short, he was able to use all his gifts. We didn't have much in way of finances so it meant a lot in more ways than one. One gift for Joey from the shower was a t-shirt that read "Jesus loves me" with a picture of Jonathan and David on the front. I think it was Joey's favorite. I know it was my favorite and Joey actually outgrew that one. It is often the little things people do that make life enjoyable and sometimes bearable in life's unpredictable challenges. A lot of what Jimmy's mother wrote about became all too true for me. No matter how hard I tried I certainly had reminders of his handicap. I had another excerpt given to me at the beginning of Joey's little stay with me. It was interesting, and I would like to share it in Joey's story.

The Special Mother by Emma Bombeck (written over 30 years ago)

Most women become mother by accident, some by choice, a few by social pressures and a couple by habit. This year nearly 100,000 women will become mothers of handicapped children. Did you ever wonder how handicapped children are chosen?

"Armstrong, Beth, son, patron saint, Matthew."

"Forest, Marjorie, daughter, patron saint, Cecelia."

Finally He passes a name to an angel and smiles. "Give her a handicapped child."

The angel is curious, "Why this one, God? She's so happy."

"Exactly," says God. "Could I give a handicapped child to a mother who does not know laughter? That would be cruel."

"But does she have patience?" asks the angel.

"I don't want her to have too much patience or she will drown in a sea of self-pity and despair. Once the shock and resentment wears off, she'll handle it. I watched her today. She has that feeling of self and independence that is so rare and so necessary in a mother. You see, the child I am going to give has his own world. She has to make it live in her world and that's not going to be easy."

"But Lord, I don't think she even believes in you."

God smiles. "No matter. I can fix that. This one is perfect. She has just enough selfishness."

The angel grasps, "Selfishness? Is that a virtue?"

God nods. "If she can't separate herself from the child occasionally, she'll never survive. Yes, here is a woman whom I will bless with a child less than perfect. She does not realize it yet, but she is to be envied. She will never take for granted a 'spoken word.' She will never consider a 'step' ordinary. When a child says 'MOMMA' for the first time she will be present at a miracle and know it when she describes a tree or a sunset to her blind child, she will see it as few people ever see my creations.

I will permit her to see clearly the things I see: ignorance, cruelty, prejudice. And allow her to rise above them. She will never be alone. I will be at her side every minute of every day of her life because she is doing my work as surely as she is here by my side."

"And what about her patron saint?" asks the angel, his pen poised in mid-air.

God smiles. "A mirror will suffice."

The End.

For me the line about saying Momma was soon to have special significance to me.

Life sure had its surprises. As is the protocol, we were referred to a genetic doctor twice, though at the time I wasn't sure why. The first visit aroused a lot of feelings, as Joey's dad was trying to argue with the doctor. It was very uncomfortable. This doctor was kind but very blunt. On the second visit, I brought Joey and held him upright as if to show him off. I had the mother's pride working. I knew Joey was perfect even if those doctors thought otherwise. God was the one I leaned on, not the specialist. I had the word of God, as Psalm 146:5 says: "Happy is he who has the God of Jacob for his help. Whose hope is in the Lord?"

The peace of God entered into those doctor visits with a very real presence. Once I sensed the Lord say, "Becky, I am the great physician and I know Joey for who he really is."

I continued to learn and grow as God is eternal and continual. It's a true, personal God that I serve. As the word of God says, "God is an ever present help in times of trouble. God words never fail."

As long as we live we still deal with feelings, but with God's grace our faithfulness overcomes feelings. God wills us to never give up. Sometimes I thought I was dreaming; fears would rise up and I thought they would never end. In reality, I was on a love walk with my Savior.

I learned to manage and attend to Joey's physical health. Joey's weak heart was the most tragic of all Joeys trails. God's goodness was given as I learned truly how important and wonderful the gift of life is no matter what crosses one may have to bear. I cannot deny how mixed up I felt sometimes. I know that it was the strength that only comes from my heavenly Father that upheld me. God held my hand and was as close as a whisper of a prayer. Even in times when I thought He left, He was there. The Lord became very real to me during Joey's brief stay with me. The word of God came alive: "Your Father knows what you need before you ask Him" (Matthew 6:8). I'd read that over and knew that there was no room to doubt that God knows what He's doing. I knew full well He would take care of me and Joey. I repeated Bible verses to strengthen myself and "God knows my needs even before I ask him" was continually on my lips.

I can remember the feeling that whatever happened to Joey happened to me. It is really true that mothers would rather take on any pain than see their children go through it.

I detested that bag on his tummy with a passion, even though I knew it saved his life. Even though the trial of teaching Joey to breastfeed was frustrating, it was tiny in comparison to the frustration I felt about the task of a colostomy. I'd make plans in my mind of what I would do when Joey no longer had the stoma.

Doctors would not satisfy me with their theories about colostomies. The doctors called it an individual thing. No one would say what I wanted to hear. Maybe this was a good thing, as I had no choice but to look to God and to trust. Therefore, I would find myself praying continually, daily, that the anus surgery Joey was to have at a year old would be successful. I wanted Joey to have the best and I knew God could do it. God's word said, "Ask and it shall be given," so I made sure to ask. I would remember all the good things God already did for me and Joey. All the little miracles that said, *I'm here*. I stood on God's promise that all things work together for the good of those who love God. I believed that all things are possible with God. '**For with God nothing is ever impossible and no word from God shall be without power or impossible of fulfillment.**"(Luke 1; 37). What I thought would be impossible became possible as I found strength for the days of Joeys challenges. (Psalm 121; 1 ;)"I will lift my eyes unto the hills, from whence cometh my help "was another scripture with which I became familiar.

I still felt it would be unfair for a boy with Down syndrome to have a colostomy for life. Then I would remind myself that Joey would not have lived without it and I had to be thankful and remember Joey was God's child first. I felt so close to Joey and having Joey was a privilege. I know he was perfect as any baby could be. The love between me and my baby needed no words. We communicated without words. We were as in love as any mother and son could be.

Everyday life became a process of trusting God for everything. I'd fretted that the colostomy bag would fall off and cause his skin to burn when we went for physiotherapy. I decided to bathe Joey just prior to physiotherapy so I could relax. Changes happened and we were given a new sure fit colostomy bag that lasted longer, another blessing where by God was just on time. I believe God was teaching me to trust him for everything.

I was thankful for science, as even the smallest effort made on improving essentials for the special needs individuals or any medical problem can make a huge difference for one's quality of life. I believe God uses medical science and research to perform His miracles. God is limitless.

I used to wonder what Joey thought of this apparatus, his stoma. Joey had this stoma since he was one day old, so I am sure he became used to it. I loved the John Denver song that went "When the River Meets the Sea." What my baby's thoughts were was a mystery to me, yet I believed Joey and I knew at times what each other were thinking. My imagination told me Joey knew more than I did about what was going on in our lives. In a sort of round-about way Joey seemed to keep the element of surprise alive. For a baby who was classed as being slow he had a way of trying to rip off his colostomy bag before I could blink an eye. Then he would scratch the stoma during bath, so I had to watch him like a hawk.

Bath times were fun; you could almost catch the joy in the air. The water and air on his stoma must have felt great and we interacted socially and spiritually. A small activity, but it was a refreshing time in the midst of all the troubles we went through. The good lord knew how much I needed refreshing.

Joey's second surgery was when he was eleven months old. This was a successful surgery, which reversed the colostomy. Consequently, Joey was granted three months with no colostomy and we had more freedom and another blessing. I no longer had the chore of caring for a stoma.

But then along came dirty diapers. For first time in my life, I welcomed the dirty diapers. It meant my baby could roll and play without a bump on his belly. I was thankful. If God was dealing with me to be thankful even for the dirty diapers, it worked. I was growing in many ways. Little or big, I welcomed all the miracles and blessings. I believe I stopped looking for some big miracle, as all the smaller ones seemed big. God really is concerned about the details in our lives and blesses us even when we're not aware.

God was as patient with me, as I must have sounded like a demanding little child when I was on my knees for Joey. I can recall praying, "Now, God, You know how extra difficult it will be for Joey because of his Downs without the chore of caring for a colostomy, so you just *have* to do something." I'm sure God had a chuckle over that one. I am sure I was professional at rationalizing how to sell ideas for God to help us out. I had to remember that we can tell God our plans but He has His plans for us already in place. Either way I am once again thankful that God never forgot me and Joey.

I was in a process of discovering some things about myself such as I can actually do some things I had been convinced were impossible for me to learn. I believe it was only possible by the grace of God. I learned how adaptable we humans can be and how we handle situations we cannot change—a real revelation. I discovered God-given abilities. I had to grow up when it came to my own self-worth and maturity. I learned to recognize what was miraculous. God used my experiences with my special needs baby to make me more mature. I came to know that with God I have what I don't have, because he gives what I lack. I recall I got so trained at doing the colostomy that I believed I was the only one who knew how. I went from one extreme to the other. I went from no worth to pride, obviously still needing to grow. I needed to get wisdom, to stand on God's word. I needed to learn more how to trust God's word.

I grew in the ways of God and matured enough to know nothing is fair all of the time. How one develops the correct attitude is what we need all the time. The attitude of "keep on walking" when one wants to give up was a tough lesson, but not impossible. It required great determination and my overused word, perseverance.

Sometimes I think of history and what lessons it holds, such as the story of Michael Angelo. About how Michael only had a block of marble when he had a vision of something bigger than anyone else and thus chipped away a masterpiece. This is what I think God wants to do in our lives, chip away the junk and have a life that's a masterpiece.

Chapter Four
Joey's Short Stay

I CAN ALWAYS REMEMBER GOD'S hand on my life. God's hand of love, comfort, and peace became more alive to me during Joey's short stay of fifteen months. Though it was too short, I remain thankful as I experienced closeness to my son that I will treasure for all time. During these fifteen months I collected poems, notes, newspaper articles, letters, bible verses, and pictures that lifted my spirits and helped me draw into God for both strength and wisdom. Long before my last two children were born, I hung a pamphlet by my bed. This pamphlet had a picture of a mom holding her baby up close to her face and the inscription on the bottom read, "Near to the Heart of God." I sensed a real presence of God when I read it for the first time and I believe it was just one of many nuggets that helped my walk with God. I saw that picture every single day prior to having Joey. I knew God was always speaking to my heart.

I knew how special children are to God and how God wants us all to know how they all hold a special place in God's heart. Every child is different, like snowflakes, and all made by our Creator.

Children are gifts from the Lord God. And to clone a snowflake would be a grave error, a sad error for us all.

Jesus said in His word, (Amplified Bible) Matthew 19:14; But he said, Leave he children alone! Allow the little ones to come unto Me, and do not forbid or restrain or hinder them, for such (as these) is the kingdom of heaven composed.

In my keeping was a poster from friends, which I also hung on the wall in my bedroom. It pictured a small child playing in the sand with a beautiful sunset in the background and the biblical inscription: "As you have done it unto the least of these you have done it unto me." That one picture spoke volumes to me, as it reinforced that children are the gifts and treasures of God, the Heavenly Father.

Another inspiring article which I kept I found in a local newspaper and I read it on the only Mother's Day that I had with Joseph. I hope all mothers come to know how important motherhood is. The article was written years ago.

"Thank God for Mothers"

Motherhood is
A time of headaches and memories
Sleepless nights with a sick child
Chasing away bad dreams
Waiting up.
Motherhood is sunny days in the park
Crunching dry leaves in the fall
Making a snowman that melts the next day
Making endless peanut butter sandwiches
Comforting the one who spilled the milk although
You have to clean it up.
Motherhood is nerve wracking, joyful, tiresome,
Fulfilling.

Motherhood likes dandelions
Knowing nursery rhymes
Kissing dirty faces.
It is applauding the first tooth and the first word
But feeling wistful at the first step.
Motherhood is teaching, healing and
Loving
It is reading the same book over and over again to
A little listener who never tires of it.
Motherhood is having a two-foot tall helper when
You would rather do it yourself.
It is the grasp of a tiny hand a radiant
Smile
And its hearing, "I wuv you Mommy" when
you really
Need it.
MOM, remember GOD LOVES YOU TOO.

Before the next Mother's Day would come around on the calendar, Joseph would be in heaven but very alive in my heart, so much so that I wrote a letter to Joey on that Mother's Day away from him. It was therapy for me to write my thoughts down. I never knew one day I would put them altogether in a book. I thought the book would be for just me but time changes things. This was the letter.

Dear Joey,

I ask myself why you were born with that hole in your heart. The doctors made me believe they could fix it, but instead you died. Joey, I know there's no doctor who can fix my heart either. Some days hurt a little, some days a lot and on this Mother's Day I hurt the most. You were my baby that I loved with all my heart and now I can only ask God's Son to heal me from losing you when you were far too young to leave or to at least help bear the pain. I love you forever, Joey. Kisses and hugs, Mom.

Thank God for all the memories. My motherhood with Joseph was surely memorable. All the memories become more vivid on remembrance days such as birthdays and death anniversaries.

Many have less troubles or ailments in a lifetime compared to Joey's fifteen months. But I want my readers to know that the personal feelings and moments are my own and not all are necessarily helpful for all moms. Some mothers gave up their child to adoption, institution, or group homes. These decisions were, I believe, done with the mother's best intentions for themselves and their child.

No one can judge the situations. I personally refuse to pass any judgment on anyone. As Gods word says: "Do not judge less you yourself be judge with the same measure." And how can someone even know what anyone has gone through unless they themselves walked in the same shoes. Many situations in life are specific to one's own personal story.

As I am writing this story of Joey, an excerpt about mothers has crossed my computer that I am going to insert. It reminds me of my own mother and may be the same for many others. We need to appreciate all mothers who went before us in this life. Imagine the extra work washing diapers on washboards. Many countries still go without our conveniences. God bless all the moms who worked so diligently despite the hardships. The following is to honor them for paving the road for us to follow.

"History of Aprons"

I don't think our kids know what an apron is or the principle use of grandma's apron was,

It was to protect the dress underneath because she only had a few.

It was also easier to wash aprons than dresses as aprons used less material.

But along with that, it served as a potholder for removing hot pans from the oven.

It was wonderful for drying children tears and on occasion was even used for cleaning out dirty ears.

From the chicken coop, the apron was used for carrying eggs, fussy chicks, and sometimes half hatched eggs to be finished in the warming oven.

With company, those aprons were ideal hiding places for shy kids.

And when the weather was cold, grandma wrapped it around her arms.

Those big old aprons wiped many a perspiring brow bent over a hot stove.

Kindling wood was brought into the kitchen in that apron.

From the garden, it carried all sorts of vegetables.

In the fall the apron was used to bring in apples.

When unexpected company drove up the road, it was surprising how much furniture that old apron could dust in a matter of seconds.

When dinner was ready grandma would walk out onto the porch, wave that apron and the men folk knew it was time to come in from the fields for dinner.

It will be a long time before someone invents something that will replace that old-time apron that seems to serve so many purposes.

Remember when grandma used that apron to set her apple pies on the window sill to cool?

Now her granddaughters set their pies on it to thaw.

And they would go crazy now trying to figure out how many germs were on grandma's apron.

Well I don't think I ever caught anything from grandma's apron

BUT LOVE

How did the previous pioneer mothers ever managed? I have my mother's old red checkered apron that I keep as a reminder of how good I really have it. I kept memorabilia tied to memories.

"Mother's memories"

Mothers never leave us
they're always on our mind.
How well she handled horses
was her favorite line.
She bragged about her garden
and how good the neighbors are.
A small town country living,
where they never owned a car.

Mom you are special, you always have been
you died a humble lady, now you are living like
a queen.
When mamma went to heaven, she did not
really die,

From a shack to a mansion, in the twinkling of
an eye.
Mom was young at heart as she spoke of her
next of kin, never getting older, just covered with
wrinkled skin.
My only regret was not being by her side
to glimpse the holy angels the moment that
she died.
If you never had a mom, there's no need to be sad.
Just put your trust in Jesus and you'll have the
neatest Dad.
He'll care for you and love you,
Just let Him have his way
And you'll meet your mom in heaven come
reunion day.

(Russell Scherer)

The story about Joey was the longest one in my life that I loved to share. I had lots to say. After all, Joey spent his first month in the hospital before I got him home and one more month in the hospital when he had the colostomy reversed, and another ten days in the hospital prior to his death, not to mention emergency visits.

I would say Joey had quite the eventful life for being here only fifteen short months but it gave me the chance to get to know my son. I'm eternally grateful as I feel I actually did come to know him in a very special way which can never fully be explained. I got to see Joey jump in his Jolly Jumper. I recall Joey jumping for long stretches repeatedly saying, "I do, I do." I loved to just sit quietly and watch Joey. The first time I sat Joey in his Jolly Jumper I went downstairs to do laundry and returned to find Joey hanging upside down. Joey was just quietly hanging upside not making one sound. Of course I quickly turned Joey right side up and sat down and laughed my head off. Joey's brother, Darren, was supposed to be keeping eye on Joey but was instead intently watching TV. We all had to laugh, as Joey was so quiet it was almost as if he enjoyed the change of view. Joey kept us on our toes, as he did the same thing the first time ever in his high chair. This time I had Joey tied nicely into the chair and with confidence left the room briefly to do the never-ending laundry, only to return in time to catch Joey slipping out the bottom. I caught him before he hit the floor or banged his head. I learned just because Joey was labeled slow didn't mean he didn't like to try new things. It didn't dampen Joey's spirits. Joey loved life and to have fun. Nothing seemed to bother Joey except when he saw a doctor or a hospital or worse yet, a needle. Otherwise Joey's disposition was always happy. Little things seemed to intrigue Joey and bring happiness. Joey seemed happier than usual whenever we went to church, as he would cheerfully babble all the way to and from church. This was music to my ears. I must say, and I may be repeating myself, but I sincerely felt that everything that I said or did with Joey was treasured moments. I did not know why, at least I had no idea at the time. I just knew everything was important and special and know God was speaking to my heart. God was saying, "Joey will be with me soon, enjoy him with all your being." I never believed it could be, because Joey's stay would be so short. This was not a possible to me, as I knew God was a good God and miracles and healing were on God's agenda. That is where I put my faith, all the faith I could muster up. Nothing else made much sense. I stood on the words *God is a good God* from the beginning. Thus, only good was to come into Joseph's life. I believed the doctors, nurses, friends, and all Joey's contacts would see miracles. I know they did, but it was not what I had in mind. I heard a remark at church one time that stayed with me and could possibly explain a lot of where I was. It went like this: "If God were small enough for our minds he wouldn't be big enough to meet our needs." How could I know and understand what all God was doing or going to do with Joey's future? I do know that I am who I am today at least in part for all I learned and experienced because of Joey.

My character and attitude is a lot different than it otherwise might have been without my snowflake. My dependence on the Lord heightened, as did the desire to read the Bible. I would relate stories in the Bible to what I was dealing with. One of those stories was the story of Joseph, who was the youngest of brothers who sold him into slavery because they were jealous of him. I thought to myself, how blind these brothers were to the plan of God for Joseph's life, as Joseph in the Bible grew to live in the ruler or king's palace. I associate the same kind of blindness with society of our day, how society has blindfolds on when it comes to Down syndrome and disabilities. Society all too often sees only the nega- tive, side. Society too often overlooks the good and in ignorance doesn't see how God wants to work out His purposes in all life. God is concerned for more than just the physical; He also develops our spiritual lives. God has a plan for each and every life. To look to God is to grow in strength, the kind of strength that only God can give. It's sad that so many could only see the Downs not the little snowflake I named Joey. Joey was a baby with Down syndrome not a Down syndrome baby. I noticed how others saw the difference first and I wanted them to see the perfectness first. I wanted them to know that Joey was God's child first, and how could that be anything but perfect? I carried a saying in my heart that read: *Don't Clone a Snowflake!*

Society still has many compassionate, sensitive people. I believe most people are basically good. Society just often lacks insight and I became very aware of it with my Joey. Change comes with knowing the Creator, "God." I would like to include part of poem I found saved in my keepsake box.

"Blind" by (John Kendrick Bangs)

"Show me your God," the doubter cries
I point him to the smiling skies
I show him all the woodland greens
I show him all the peaceful sylvan scenes
I show him winter snow and frosts
I show him waters tempest-tossed
I show him hills rock-ribbed and strong;
I bid him hear the thrushes' song;
I show him flowers in the close—
The lily, violet and rose
I show him rivers, babbling streams
I show him youthful hopes and dreams
I show him stars, the moon, and the sun,
I show deeds of kindness done,
I show him joy, I show him care
And still he holds his doubting air,
And faithless goes his way
For he is blind of soul and cannot see!

As many become educated, awareness grows. Choosing to lean into the things of God, blindness dwindles and wisdom grows. Criticism for anyone classified as handicapped becomes secondary and potential is emphasized. Opened eyes see many stories of success; stories that build faith, brotherhood, and acceptance. I saw a television program where the star of the show was an individual with Down syndrome. Obviously, the individual had a full, productive life. We learn from many Down syndrome children the meaning of unconditional love, as they desire to please. Other programs on television educate society. Teachers were being interviewed and said the actor with Down syndrome was very good and did not want to perform unless he was very sure of himself and his lines.

The actors who worked with the individual with Down syndrome also said they were very impressed. Any obvious limitations were not an issue for this person with Down syndrome. Maybe the actor was the blessed one because no one ever told him he couldn't achieve success and therefore he believed in himself.

It is us as a society that needs to change and rid ourselves of a negative attitude, not ignoring the realistic limitations but instead always remaining positive. Knowing our own potential can be a problem, so how we can judge others' potential?

I spent time watching children programs like Sesame Street when I had three young children at home. Often there were children with Down syndrome participating. And all the other children accepted and treated them as equals. We can learn a lot from children. We just need to remember that in reality, the only handicapped child is one deprived of love. I believe God is love and to really truly love we must accept God's love for us. God is the author and finisher, the almighty Creator!

Busy became my middle name during Joey's short stay with his family. How I found the time to read and tend to all the basic things was a challenge, and then Christmas rolled around. At church, individuals were asked to bring something to share for a small Christmas service. I decided to share a testimonial. I didn't know, of course, that this was the one and only Christmas Joey would share with us.

First Chickenpox then Christmas

Joey was four months old at the time. It is as follows.

I believe my testimony is a Christmas gift to everyone. I want to share thoughts about Joey and how I feel Joey was meant to be from the beginning of time. In the Bible, Ephesians 1:4, it reads: "Accordingly as he hath chosen us in Him before the foundation of the world." And I also believe Joey was no accident but created the way he is by God. In the Bible, Exodus 11 reads: "And the Lord said who make the dumb, the deaf, or the seeing or the blind? Have not I the Lord." Some of you may say to yourself, *but Joey is handicapped.* Would God do that? I can't answer all the questions. I only know what God says in his word. I think we also have to look at how we define handicapped. We all here know Joey has a condition called Down syndrome, but I can tell you that even as a baby, Joey has the ability to love in ways that many of us cannot because of the many masks we wear. I have to ask, which is the greater handicap? Could it be that our masks are an even greater handicap? To illustrate my point I want to share a story given to me by Joey's infant development teacher, Fran. Fran said that she and her son were at a swimming pool when a child with Down syndrome was yelling her son's name from across the other side of the pool. Fran said her son became embarrassed. Fran explained to her son that the girl with Down syndrome did this only because she was so happy to see him. And to think about how many people are always that happy to see you. Her son was no longer so embarrassed when he understood.

In this story, we see the girl with Down syndrome had no mask on, which is what many of us wish we could be like. I feel that Joey will teach my family and others during his life many things in like fashion of the story I just shared. I believe Joey will be blessed in his life, as I already have been blessed in his four months. I have become more and more close to God. I have become more appreciative of little things. I feel like a mother whose son just won the Olympic gold when Joey gave me his first smile. Many mothers take it for granted when their child nurses, but for me it was a miracle from God. The doctors said, "Joey's sucking is the pits." But I kept trying. Each time I went to the hospital to nurse Joey, I left depressed as I met with no success to nurse Joey. I'd leave thinking it wasn't worth it. But God entered my thoughts with a satisfying peace. It was my experience that when we pray for specifics God hears, so I prayed; and despite challenging obstacles and the doctor's attitude, Joey and I, became a happy nursing couple. I gave God the thanks and I know God will continue to help as Joey gives life a meaning. I am looking forward to life with Joey as a part of our family. I admit I had mixed feelings when Joey was first born and I had time to think the first month with Joey's hospital stay. But then I needed to accept the health problems and a handicapped child as part of my life. Now he holds my heart. I once thought the worst thing that could happen to me would be to have a child labeled retarded. Yet now I cannot express my happiness and love for my baby Joseph. Despite the imperfections in the world's eyes, he is perfect in my eyes and I love him greatly. Because of this special love I feel for

Joey, I have to reflect on how much Jesus must love us despite our imperfections. I feel all the prayers from loved ones and friends, and come into the fullness of how God hears and answers prayers. How God is always there for us. If I thought for a moment this life was all there was, I suppose Joey's life may seem hopeless, but I thank the Lord there is a greater life in the hereafter and Joey is here to help me prepare for it. In the meantime, I intend to live life daily like every day is a new beginning. As the famous hymn says:

> When peace like a river, attendeth my way,
> When sorrows like sea billows roll:
> Whatever my lot, Thou has taught me to say;
> It is well; it is well, with my soul. (Horatio Spafford)

I believe God wants us to look to him for answers and do our best with whatever situations life gives us. And Joey has been called exceptional; maybe so but maybe he had a special purpose. Throughout all my life I know the Lord is good and kind to us all, so let us rejoice this Christmas. Let's enjoy the beautiful fresh snowfalls, little snowflakes, and I quote (Phil. 4:6–7)"And the peace of God, which transforms all understanding, will guard your hearts and your minds in Christ Jesus." Merry Christmas!

The above testimonial was shared at a Christmas church service a long time ago, long before I decided to put Joe's story on paper and long before I knew the title "Don't Clone a Snowflake." Much time has passed; I have since had twenty-three years working as a caregiver for special needs individuals. Not all my ideas have remained the same. For example, I have used the term "retarded" in my testimonial, which is no longer politically correct. More acceptable terms or words for handicapped individuals include challenged, special needs, or exceptional. Personally, I believe the attitude and deliverance behind the word when used is what really matters. When one uses words like idiot and dummy, they are often ridiculing others. Yet even then a proper attitude can change the deliverance, which will also affect a response. Even positive words with wrong attitude or deliverance can be ridiculing. When I used the word retarded in my testimonial, it was about a baby I loved more than I can express and I would never even entertain the idea of insulting him. Attitudes have a way of spilling over into every area of our lives and relationships. People can sense what one means to say without always being politically correct with choice of words. Well-meaning people go overboard with labels and the correct word, and without realizing it make differences even more obvious. Society knows what mentally challenged means. I believe if society accepted and loved individuals with differences and handicaps, labels would not be an issue in the first place. I suppose I'm a bit of a dreamer because that would mean we would live in a perfect world. So I believe the real challenge is to teach society that it is okay to be slow, handicapped, or different in some way, and it should not be the focus to fix and change but instead to accept and love.

The story of Joey laid a strong foundation in my life. Though many times I have questioned God, I have concluded that I don't know all that goes on in the spiritual side of life; that's God's business. The Bible says in Rev. 22:13, "I am the Alpha and the Omega, the Beginning and the End, the first and the last."

God is divine, supernatural, unending, eternal, and constant. God's healing is continual, as he is eternal. Joey's healings were ongoing and not always instant, and even if I didn't understand it all, God is faithful to bring understanding in due time as I lean unto Him, almighty God.

One story I heard in a sermon years ago that totally made sense regarding the understanding of how God works in the supernatural and how much God loves us went as follows:

A family man was asked to go to church. His family pleaded with him saying, "It's Christmas, just come with us as a family activity." The man flatly refused saying, "I would be a hypocrite if I go to church." When the family asked him why he answered with, "Because I just cannot believe any God would make himself a man and he would become a man. I just can't. I can't believe that." So the family left without the man and went to church. He stayed at home and lit a fire and settled down to relax for the evening when he heard birds flying into his window. He thought the birds must have seen the fire, so he quickly ran out to chase them away, but some were already dead or injured. Then he ran to find something to cover the window but nothing seemed to work very well. So, the man thought to himself, I wish I could become a bird long enough to talk to them in their talk so they would stop hurting themselves. All of a sudden, he had a flash as though a light went on and he realized that's why God became a man. It was to show us the way. That was why we have Christmas today. Jesus came as a baby and grew into a man and died on the cross to save mankind.

The story about the family man and birds was a simple explanation to demonstrate God's love for mankind. The story is about a God too big to ever understand in mankind terms, though God fixes that, too. My mind cannot fully conceive God's bigness. I have to lean unto God, understanding and trusting he will reveal what I need to know in his timing. Thirty years have flown by since Joe's passing, but time did not change my love of a little snowflake and all he taught me.

Yesterday I was at the gym and saw two ladies who I hadn't seen in years. They looked older and I had to say to myself, "No way has that much time flown by." I believe no one can deny life as we know it passes all too quickly. Life is a vapor, as Bible states in James 4:14: "For what is your life? It is even a vapor that appears for a little time and then vanishes away." So I had even a smaller vapor pass me by with Joey's life. I had to stretch quickly, grow quickly. Fifteen months was hardly enough time to catch my breath. It was a crash course on so many things. I had to do a lot of exercising regarding God as my source. Joey was God's child on loan to me. So there was no giving up. Trusting in God's love brought me back to my feet to walk through my struggles. I came to the understanding that valleys or low places in our life aren't meant to hold us down but instead to help us grow. Valleys are to be a temporary address, not a place to park, as that's when depression sickness can set in. I just kept walking. I knew Joey and Jesus loved me, so I would rise up my banner of faith and lean more into the God, as I knew him to be love. I would read scriptures such as Peter 1:6–9(Amplified bible) "(You should) be exceedingly glad on this account, though now for a little while you may be distressed by trails and suffer temptations. So that (the genuineness) of your faith may be tested, (your faith) which is more precious than perishable gold which is tested and purified by fire. (This proving of your faith is intended) to rebound to (your) praise and glory and honor when Jesus Christ (the Messiah, the Anointed One) is revealed. Without having seen Him, you love Him; though you do not (even) now see Him, you believe in Him and exult and thrill with inexpressible and glorious and (triumphant, heavenly)joy.(At the same time)you receive the result(outcome, consummation)of your faith, the salvation of your souls."

I knew that trials did strengthen my faith and often times overcoming challenges with God were demonstrations of God's love for me. Sometimes I would just think of a Bible verse for the day and often it would be a simple word that would get me through: "God loves me."

Walking with God is an adventure. God is a big good God full of surprises, hope, and joy. God wants to give us hope. Jeremiah 29:11 says, "For I know the plans I have for you, says the Lord, thoughts of peace and not of evil, to give you a future and a hope." Sounds like an adventure to me! The Holy Spirit gave me hope. I cannot imagine how people get through the hard times without the Lord. The truth is, Jesus is ever present in the times of trouble and makes the good times even better if we invite Him into our lives. I had hope for a future for Joey's life. I believed all his tomorrows would be better than all his yesterdays. I believe the word of God in that He has plans for everyone and gives the world hope. All creation should be valued. God loves His creation. Genesis 1:31:"Then God saw everything He had made and indeed it was very good."

God's love is eternal. And my Love for Joey is eternal. Love from above is as unexplainable as it is perfect. I would like to include this beautiful song by Phil Driscoll:

"What Kind of Love is this?"

Well I used to think that Jesus was just some kind
of imagination,
And I used to think that He possibly could
have lived.
But I never cared how He died or understood why,
Thought it didn't matter anyway
That kind of love is this?
That a man should give His life on a wooden cross,
He gave His life for His friends
What kind of love is this?

Now I know that Jesus, He had a plan before He
came here,
Came from beyond the stars out in space,
To a world that was bound up with chains
of darkness
He spilled His blood just to set us free,
What kind of love is this?
That a man would give His life on a wooden cross
He gave His life for His friends.

What kind of love is this?
What kind of LOVE?

I learned God's love works in the invisible. I learned that in God's world life is to be lived one day at a time, as tomorrow has plans of its own. I learned through a short fifteen months of dealing with health issues that growing in God's love was all part of having my Down syndrome baby. God's arm of love extended itself over all the problems. Love came through friends with such heart-felt motives, comfort, and ministry. As the saying goes, a man who has a friend who they can count on is rich indeed. Another saying, a man without patience is poor indeed. I'm not sure who originally said either, but I'm happy Joe taught me some patience and most times I feel rich from inside out.

One day my special friend, Lona, called me up on the phone. Lona's enthusiasm on the phone was filled with sheer excitement as she shared with me her plans, saying, "Let's hurry and go. David Mainse and his group from TV, a cast of *100 Huntley*, are having breakfast downtown, so let's go and meet him and maybe get some prayers for Joey." Well, she didn't have to ask me twice. I was a regular viewer of the *100 Huntley* program so I agreed to hurry and go. It was Joey's bath day, which entailed a colostomy bag change so I had to postpone and pray the bag would not loosen while we were out. Quick as I could, I packed up all the necessities for Joey and his sister, who still needed diapers. It was a lot of preparation but I was thrilled at the prospect of getting out of the house. We arrived at the restaurant just in time. At first we were unable to spot David Mainse, the leader of *100 Huntley*, so Lona wandered off to get us our much needed coffee and fresh muffins, which was doubly special for me, as not only was I getting out of the house but someone else was serving me coffee.

A lady just across from my table exchanged smiles with me and headed over to me to visit. Immediately she began admiring Joey and I went into download babble. While enjoying the brief conversation, I turned to see David Mainse walking my way. I silently whispered, "Lord let this man pray for Joey." As David walked by, this stranger interrupted his course and relayed our conversation to him. With hardly a "hello," David proceeded to lay his hands upon Joseph's little head and whispered a prayer. The prayer was short in words but overflowing in the spirit of the presence of almighty God. The inexpressible divine sense of God's pure love seemed to flow off of David's hands and fill the atmosphere. All I recall being said was, "Dear sweet Jesus." I remember thinking, He sees Jesus in Joey's eyes too and how appropriate to address the prayer with such personal words with respect to the preciousness of God's love. I was grateful, as I experienced another foretaste of life hereafter and how sweet it will be.

The experience gave my faith a boost and I chose to believe in more miracles for Joey. I believe Joey had a miracle that day, as he was quite strong physically when one considers how much strength he needed to keep up with that rapid heartbeat and a heart with a big hole in the center. I received a sense of preciousness of life itself that day. Love was something I came into with more and more deepness. It turned out to be quite a day; I was thankful for Lona's thoughtfulness that day. Another highlighted day—in Joey's short fifteen months on earth, he fit in a personal prayer with a television personality. That's my boy!

The pain that I had in wanting to fix Joey's health issues was ongoing, but with the pain came the blessing of Joey's catchy happiness. It was contagious like a virus. I would always feel such happiness whenever I was cuddling my baby Joey. My faith grew and I expected a great future for baby Joey and knew he would receive a full, happy, meaningful life with Jesus by his side. In some respects, it was easy for me to have faith, as I cannot over emphasize how much I sensed God's abounding love during Joey's life. I would see with my natural eyes things like Joey's low muscle tone, some bodily floppiness and other Down syndrome characteristics, but in my spiritual eyes I saw perfection and I had peace that surpassed all understanding. The Bible verse in Philippians 4:6–7 was a truth I grew into as I leaned unto God in prayer. The verse read, "Be anxious for nothing, but in everything by prayer and supplication, with thanksgiving, let your requests be made known to God, which surpasses all understanding, will guard your hearts and minds through Christ Jesus." And God did just that for me.

Everything circled back to my relationship with the Lord. I realized that God is more interested in my character than my reputation. My reputation is what people think I am, but my character is what God knows I am. The truth is I will grow in character, or in the image of Christ according to His will, as I grow in my relationship with the Lord personally.

Chapter 5
Love Relationship

I JOHN 4:16 SAID,(NEW LIVING Translation) "We know how much God loves us, and we have put our trust in his love. God is love and all who live in love live in God, and God lives in them. And as we live in God, our love grows more perfect."

I have learned I am never alone. I am sure many readers have read the article or poem called "One Night I had a Dream." The story is about someone talking to the Lord in a dream and they said:

"Lord, you said that once I decided to follow you, you would walk with me all the way. But I have noticed that during the most troublesome times in my life, there is only one set of footprints. I don't understand why in times that I needed you most, you would leave." The Lord replied: "My precious child, I would never leave you during your times of trail and suffering, when you see only one set of footprints, it was then that I carried you."

The story is about believing God is with you even when you may think He is not.

11 Corinthians 5; 7 ;(Amplified bible), **For we walk by faith (we regulate our lives and conduct ourselves by our**

conviction or belief respecting mans relationship to God and divine things, with trust and holy fervor; thus we walk) not by sight or appearance.

I had a measure of faith to believe in things that were not yet a reality. I "knew" someone greater than me was holding my hand; just as I read in "One Night I had a Dream," Jesus' love is always and forever.

On my own I know I would have crumbled under the circumstances of Joey's health issues. It took faith. As I walked and believed, I became stronger in my faith. Through the struggles my faith was stretched. Like a tree in a storm my roots had to go deeper into the things of God to grow and all while leaning into my relationship with almighty God, the Creator and Savior of mankind. I had to remember,

To live in the present while having hope for a future is God's plan.

"Be still and know He is God" means to rest in Him. He knows what He is doing we only need to trust. People over complicate so much of God's word. We can trust when we fully know God holds the trump card. In Matthew 6:33 it says, "But seek you first the kingdom of God and His righteousness and all these things shall be added unto you. Therefore, do not worry about tomorrow for tomorrow will worry about its own things. Sufficient for the day is its own trouble."

The Bible is a manual on love as it is the living word of God.

Joey's life was learning to lean on and trust the Lord. I needed someone to lean on and who better than the Lord?

The Bible says to be fruitful, grow in faith. (Women of Destiny Bible) 11 Peter 1:5 says, "Giving all diligence, add to your faith virtue, to virtue knowledge, self-control, to self-control, brotherly kindness, and to brotherly kindness love." God wants everyone to grow in faith by trusting Him. Little by little we grow.

I was given a gift when Joey was born and that gift was called "not giving up," as I never gave up on God or Joey.

I believed from the beginning of Joey's life that I served a good God and who could ever give up on a precious little *snowflake* like my Joey.

The Bible says in Genesis 1, "In the beginning God created the heavens and the earth was without form, and void, and darkness was on the face of the deep. And the spirit of God was hovering over the face of the waters. Then God said let there be light and there was light." And in verse 27 it goes on to say, "So God created man in His own image: in the image of God he created them." So, we see from the Bible that God just had to give His word and it was done. God made the world and he made Joey. God's creativity made us all different and special. Think how creative God must be to make us in His image, yet give us all different finger prints. With everyone being different it stands to reason that we all would have different jobs to do.

Big mistake to clone a snowflake!

Everyone has a spot to fill or a special job to do, even if it is one single thing. We just need to become the best in what we already are. God has a glorious plan and purpose for every individual to grow as His creation.

We are all a work in progress. Faith needs a foundation to grow and in valleys one has to exercise faith and so we grow. God wants us to have good things filled with His blessings. In 3 John 1:3 it says, "Beloved I pray that you may prosper and be in health, just as your soul prospers." Obviously God intends struggles to be temporary.

A song titled "A Piece of the Rock by Sammy Hall is one of my favorites. The words are "I got a piece of the rock no longer building on sand, daily with Jesus I walk."

Walking in a love relationship with God I received the out-pouring of God's love through many divine appointments. New friends were instrumental in growing spiritually.

In 1 John 3:16–18, it tells of God's love and reads as follows: "By this we know love, because He laid down His life for us. And we also ought to lay down our lives for the brethren. But whoever has these worlds' goods, and sees his brother in need, and shuts his heart from him, how does the love of God abide in him? My little children let us not love in word or in tongue, but in deed and in truth." God's agenda for love is to practice what we preach or else love is meaningless. Joey gave the word "love" new meaning, just as my and Joey's song says in the start of this book.

Another amazing story I heard once upon a time at a church service goes as follows: In our congregation, we had an individual with Down syndrome who wanted a job in our church, so he was given the job to pass out hymn books at the door of the sanctuary when people entered. Prior to this one particular Sunday, a member of the church had lost his wife. The elders and members were at a loss as what to say or do for the man whose wife had just died. Yet the adult man with Down syndrome had no reservations and when he saw the grieving man he just walked over to him, gave him a big hug and repeated, "I am so sorry." The amazing part of the story is that no one had bothered to tell the Down syndrome individual that the man had lost his wife. He had no knowledge regarding the loss the man had endured.

Obviously, the man passing out the hymn books had some sensitivity that no one else was aware. Maybe this individual was just fulfilling his special job. It's good to note that the only thing that could have been done was done by the man who handed out hymn books, and that was to hand out love. The individual followed his heart, without hesitation, without any thought to whether it was right or wrong. I suppose that in part the adult man with Downs had a child-like mind whereby everyone is a friend yet to be discovered. Maybe that's why in Mark 10:14–15, Jesus' words are "Let the little children come unto Me, and do not forbid them for such is the kingdom of heaven. Assuredly I say unto you whosoever does not receive the kingdom of God as a little child will by no means enter into it." I believe God is talking here about child-like faith.

I found a prayer I am going to include, as it sheds a light on a real personal God that is by an unknown author. It is as follows:

"God's Prayer to Men"

You do not have to be clever to please me; all you have to do is want to love me.

Just speak to me as you would to anyone of whom you are very fond of.

I long to talk with you.

Are there any people you want to pray for? Say their names to me, and ask of me as much as you like. I am generous and I know all their needs, but I want you to show your love for them and for me by trusting me to do what I know is best.

Tell me about the poor, the sick, the sinners, and if you have lost the friendship or affection of anyone, tell me about that, too.

Is there anything you want for your soul? If you like you can write out a long list of all your needs, and come and read it to me.

Just tell me about your pride, your touchiness, self-centredness, meanness and laziness. Do not be ashamed; there are saints in heaven that had the same faults, yet they prayed to me and little by little they overcame their faults.

Do not hesitate to ask me for blessings for the body and mind; for health, money success. I can give you everything, and I always give everything to make your souls holier.

What is it that you want today? I long to do you good. What are your plans? I yearn to bless them. Tell me about them. Is there anyone you want to please? What is it you want to do for them?

And is there something you want to do for me? Do you want to do good for the souls of your friends who perhaps have forgotten me? Tell me about your failures and I will show you the cause of them so you may overcome them. What are your worries? Who has caused you pain? Tell me about it all and add that you will forgive and forget and I will bless you.

Are you afraid of anything? Have you any tormenting, unreasonable fears? Trust yourself to Me. I am here. I see everything will not leave you.

Have you no joys to tell me about? Share your happiness with me? Tell me what has happened since yesterday to cheer and comfort you. Whatever it was, however big, however small, I prepared it.

Come away with me soon. Get on with my work. Try to be quieter, humbler, more submissive, kinder, and bring me a more devoted heart. Tomorrow I will have even more blessings for you.

I shall not say good-bye, for I have promised to never leave you.

James 4:8 says, **"Draw near to God and He will draw near to you." The prayer above confirms to me how God wants a relationship with people.** Yet God remains a Heavenly Father who allows free choices. God does not want mankind to be puppets but to come to Him of their own free choice and is eager to welcome all with open arms and eternal love. God's love is all powerful. Romans 8:37–39 tells me: "Despite all these things, overwhelming victory is ours through Christ, who loved us. And I am convinced that nothing can ever separate us from God's love. Neither death nor life, neither angels nor demons, neither our fears for today nor our worries about tomorrow, not even the powers of hell can separate us from God's love. No power in the sky above or in the earth below—indeed, nothing in all creation will ever be able to separate us from the love of God that is revealed in Christ Jesus our Lord." That's the Bible.

God's love is better than any insurance policy that I have ever heard of; a cannot be changed policy, lasting forever. God's love relationship is His will for us.

Sometimes I was guilty of seeking miracles instead of the miracle maker, God the Father. One can have nothing materially yet have everything. Some of the happiest people in the world know God as their Father yet own very little of anything.

In life we get caught up in the doings and cares of the world. I did at times when Joey was with me. There always seemed to be so much to do. I was so busy that a year flew by and it was time for Joey's colostomy reversal.

During that first year, Joey contracted the flu twice, a cold, and the chicken pox, on top of the three surgeries, five jet rides, a host of consultations, and several hospital visits and hospital stay-over's. One silver lining was that the chickenpox came and left before Joey's one and only Christmas with his family. That was a big relief, as the chicken pox brought its own bit of trauma as Joey's stoma started to bleed and he had to visit the emergency room at the hospital. We were relieved to find out the bleeding was only a side-effect of the chicken pox. That was Joey's short life, just get over one event and another one was coming around the corner.

Joey's hospital stays for the colostomy reversal entailed a month stay for both Joey and I. The hospital arranged for me to have a bed-chair at Joey's bedside. It was a fairly comfy bed and so we settled in best we could in our hotel hospital room. Joey's daddy came for a visit. He couldn't stay long but at least he got a peek at what happens at the hospital and Joey's dad, John, took me for a drive for a change of scenery. As we drove along through streets of the city of Vancouver, we listened to the radio and the song "What a Difference You Made in My Life" music to my soul.

When all too soon Joey's funeral came along, that very song had left my memory, but not God's. By coincidence someone decided to sing it at Joey's funeral. Surely the Lord thinks of everything. The song became my love song to Joe.

Another day Grandpa visited Joey. Joe was confined to his hospital crib due to the surgery but when he heard his grandpa's voice he managed to turn his head to see his grandpa and flashed him the biggest, happiest smile. The kind of smile that would have won a smiling contest. Joey just had a perfect smile that needed no words. I loved it! Both Grandpa and I exclaimed, "Joey knows where he's at!" And I think he did. He was in the hospital but with loved ones. That was the last time Joey and Grandpa saw each other alive as the next time would be in the same hospital where Joey passed away. Joey's grandpa could not bring himself to see Joey after the heart surgery. He wanted to wait till he was better, but of course Joey did not get better that time.

Nonetheless, we did survive the hospital time that August and although Joey's visit with his grandpa was as brief as it was happy and memorable, I have to think to myself that Joey was doing the Heavenly Father's business during our hospital stay because he still shared happiness and love despite his obvious suffering.

The pain of simply not being able to hold Joey when he needed comforting had its own brand of sadness. In his hospital crib he was held in a position that kept him in one place. I could only caress and talk to him. But in the all too soon future, Joey would be sitting on Jesus' knee. What a comfort I had at that thought. I held it in my mind many a lonely moment. I imagined Joey walking and talking with Jesus. I remembered my own walks with Joey on the hospital grounds. Fresh air was doctor's orders for Joey's recovery from the colostomy reversal surgery. Joey's buttocks had diaper rash, yet this was welcomed as it meant no more colostomy.

The open air brought healing to Joey's skin and healing to my heart. I felt normal pushing my baby in a buggy around the park-like grounds. The fresh air and sunshine brought freshness to my mind that four walls in a hospital room could not bring. It felt like heaven was our ceiling. Joey and I shared some precious alone time that separated us from the gloom of more doctor visits, more needles, and the sight of white coats that came to make both Joey and I shudder. Sometimes when that needle came by to offer pain relief we both felt the pain before it even was given. Pain was not a stranger for Joey. One day when a nurse simply walked into the room to leave fresh diapers, Joey glared at me and let out a scream. His look said, "Momma don't leave me," accompanied by a look of sheer helplessness. I gave Joey a hug and soft words, which soothed his apprehension. Joey responded eagerly and soon radiated his catchy happiness again.

I have imagined that Joey could have been the author on happiness and if he would have been able to write a poem about happiness, it may have been something like this:

"Happiness"

Happiness is a smiling face looking back at you,
Like my grandpa.
Happiness is smiling eyes and a warm heart to
hold you,
Like my mom.
Happiness is bringing smiles even when in pain,
Like I do.
Happiness wants everyone else to smile even in
the rain.
I do and I get even happier as everyone wonders,
"What am I up too?"

(And I'll sign it for him): BY JOEY.

P.S. Mom, there are no handicaps in heaven.

I for one did often wonder, "What are you up to, Joey?" when he had that radiant smile.

Life went on at the hospital. We enjoyed new friends in both staff and roommates. God opened doors to share His love. I would talk about Jesus and in return people just seemed to love on us. The nurses would often remark how Joey was the best baby on the hospital floor. Being the proud mom I was, I chimed in completely. My heart would just puff up, as I was very proud of Joey.

At the hospital we felt a bond with others who had heartaches or illness. I lost a lot of my shyness with the birth of Joseph, as I felt that I had some special calling to stand up for my snowflake and all the special snowflakes in the world.

Nurses and doctors no longer intimidated me in anyway. Joey had few different thoughts, whenever a doctor would come by in one of those white uniforms Joey would yell out before they would get even near enough to touch him. The association of white uniforms with pain was Joey's signal to scream. I began to dread the doctor's visits as I knew Joey's responses. It was all part of Joey's life.

Hospitals meant pain for Joe. Joey had a cauterization surgery on his thigh. It needed to be covered with a large bandage, as the surgery required a tube be inserted into Joey's large vein which could bleed easily. This cauterization surgery was for a test wherein dye was shot into Joey's vein in order to do an examination. The bandage stayed on a number of days. When it came time for the nurse to change the bandage I was not prepared. With the removal of the bandage came a large flow of blood spurting straight out high into the air. The nurse worked quickly but I was stunned as I was instructed to hold down the bandage tightly while she readied the new one. I don't know how I managed to stand as that stream of blood flying through the air made my hair stand on end. All I can say is God blesses all the nurses who deal with blood and needles and have to answer to the doctors and deal with families from all walks of life. I respect for them for their professionalism and compassion.

It seemed like we were always waiting. Since Joey's birth, I had waited a year for the colostomy reversal surgery. What many took for granted would now become a blessing, not to ever again be taken for granted. It's hard to image for most people but I was elated when I saw Joey pass his first stool normally. I felt like I won the lotto and hollered out in joy even though the hospital room was full of visitors at the time. And I could not contain my excitement, yelling, "Joey pooped!" Along came a nurse, asking what the problem was. I explained that nothing was wrong but my baby had his first bowel movement through the normal channel. A happy moment soon followed by skin burning, a nasty rash, and medications to help Joey get comfortable.

Nurses made Joey's stay at hospital as good as possible under the uncomfortable circumstances. They amused Joey with different toys to redirect some of the pain he endured and to forget that bed was his lot in life for a month. We made a mobile out of whatever toys we had available, mostly replicas of doctors' instruments, such as a stethoscope, high blood pressure reader, and thermometer. Joey spent endless hours pulling on his mobile toy. Joey would amuse us by grabbing the nurses' and doctors' stethoscope before they knew what he was up to, as though he was saying, "Hey, what you all doing with my toys?" We all had to chuckle as Joey's reaction was quicker than the doctor's eye. Joey was going through the normal teething problems and some of those hospital items had his teeth marks on them. No one cared as long as Joey was amused. We were all happy when Joey was happy. On Joey's last day in hospital he managed to lay hold of a stethoscope and no one had the heart to take it back from him. Joey had a keepsake. I suppose he must have figured he deserved it. I know I did. Joey could not even sit on his mom's lap to be nursed when he was in pain. Joey did his time when it came to physical pain in his little life. But God was there and I know He hurt for Joey and helped with speedy healing. We were one step ahead when it came to Joey healing as God was in it.

It was another lesson on not taking anything for granted. A month later and a cuddle felt heavenly. Even though Joey's anus was still healing and I had to be careful how I held him in my arms, I was thrilled to pieces to have him so close to me. I cannot imagine what life would have been like to never have had Joey or to have given him up. Despite everything good times are treasures forever.

We had the love of Jesus ever-present. At the hospital, Joe met Erin. Erin was given the crib right next to Joseph's. We were all close from day one. Erin only wanted to be held by her mom just like Joey did. She couldn't be because her legs were up in traction and she was confined to her crib the same as Joey. It was heart breaking. I had to wonder what Erin thought when she saw Joey return from anus surgery with his legs up in traction just like hers. Joe and Erin had a lot in common with pain, but the good news was that they both had praying moms.

Moms' prayers covered everything. The day arrived for Erin's surgery and for a cast to be put on her leg. The surgery wasn't scheduled until noon, which meant it would be so long for little Erin to fast. We prayed and Erin's surgery was moved two hours sooner.

I prayed for everything during that month and surgery did go well but not without concern on the doctors' part. I reassured the doctors that I would be praying for them and the surgery. They just smiled and said thanks. When it came time for the doctors' first consultation just after the surgery their words were, "Keep up whatever you are doing because it's working and we can hardly believe how well it went." I gave God praise, as even the healing was quick according to the doctor. Initially Joey had the stoma or lump on his tummy to save his life. He had to deal with it every time he rolled on his tummy. With the lump gone after surgery came that indescribable grin the look of pure joy. His legs had been up in traction for a lengthy time.

Every time someone slipped up and bumped his bed he would holler out a loud scream. Pain killers seemed to help, but only so much. It was quite a relief when the intravenous stopped and oral pills were substituted, as by that time Joey's legs were tender and bruised due to the needles. Babies seem to be able to withstand a lot of pain, yet moms cry, pray, and try to comfort. I could see the pain in Joey's eyes and I hurt, too.

God saw his son Jesus on the cross. That, I cannot even fathom. Jesus really did pay the ultimate price by letting His son die for our sins, all because of His love for His children.

I thank God that we have a Savior and for what He did for me. That kind of love is supernatural, the kind that becomes normal when we pass it on in everyday life. The night that Jesus hung on the cross must have been the longest night for God the Father.

The night of Joey's surgery was definitely one of my longest nights ever. I just had to stand by and watch intravenous tubes hanging everywhere for Joey to receive food, fluids, and pain relievers. Often with Down syndrome comes the trait of smaller veins which was true for Joey. Consequently, Joey received more bruising from the prodding to insert the intravenous tubes. It was a lot to absorb. I tried to bring comfort by gently rubbing Joey's check, talking quietly to him to reassure him I was right there. When I did this, Joey would not cry. That was a long night, as the only time Joey would stop crying is when I was touching his face. If I left to go to the washroom, Joey would scream in agony. The following day I expressed my experience to the doctor, thinking that maybe Joey needed different pain medications. But the doctor told me that the soothing effect of caressing Joey's check actually helped Joey produce his own morphine in his body to ease his pain. I was surprised to learn of how miraculous our bodies have been designed. Sometimes mothers cannot get medicine for their sick child and still they are helping by just rubbing the cheek. I thought, "Wow, God thinks of everything." That made my day, as I was no longer just standing by watching. Mothers can do more than they are aware they can.

I was serving a good God. That night was long but I was blessed with a compassionate nurse who couldn't do enough for me and Joey. A simple gesture of bringing coffee was received gratefully. And then there was Erin's mom close by for support that night, as Erin was in pain the same night as Joey.

That night I also came to understand more of God's promise in His word. In Matthew 11:28–30, Jesus said, "Come unto Me all those who labor and heavy laden and I will give you rest. Take my yoke upon you and learn from Me, for I am gentle and lowly in heart, and you will find rest for your souls. For My yoke is easy and my burden is light." Jesus was there for us all that long night at the hospital. We had each other for support and a helpful nurse, and were blessed with some humor through it all. Proverbs 17:22 says, "A merry heart does good like medicine." It was a miracle we could laugh away some of our troubles that long night. I did a lot of no-nonsense joking to pass the time and to raise our spirits. We had to maintain ourselves in order to help our babies. Our nurse was our personal angel, and we all know angels do God's work, and she watched over us that night.

When Erin left we missed them but we got her window spot. Staring up at the sky at night and watching all the stars gave me a sense of freedom and peace, like I was looking into God's heavenly ceiling. Gazing at the stars endlessly I would drift off to sleep in the security of knowing there was a great God. God held all those stars in place and the heavens together with His awesome power. As it says in Jeremiah 10:12–13: "He has made the earth by His power, He has established the world by His wisdom, And He has stretched out the heavens by His discretion."

I loved the quiet times before a child would be crying out in the hospital. I considered it a privilege to pray for all the sick children in the hospital. I believed Jesus prayed for me and so what an honor to pray for His precious little ones. In the praying I was getting to know my God, as prayers are divine conversations with a divine supernatural creator. I had many things to just thank Him for: faithful friends, good nurses, and simple peace in the midst of turmoil. Above all, I gave thanks for His love.

God and His love are real. I remember one day feeling lonelier than I had been for a while and whispering a silent prayer for a visitor. The timing was perfect, as no sooner said than done, two ladies from my church walked in inviting me to go for a coffee. That was my secret hope that day. God read my mind or God was just being God, as Matthew 6:8 says, "*Your Father knows your needs before you ask Him.*"

I believe God just followed me around, waiting for a chance to shower down His blessings and teach me to trust Him more. God is a special love-relationship.

Joey was my special gift from God. Joey's laughter came from the bottom of his belly with a contagious smile. Watching Joey blow bubbles was very entertaining as he did it with such enthusiasm. It was as if he was practicing for a big debut, thoroughly enjoying himself in the process. Joey's eyes were what stole the show as they had that glimpse of the love of Jesus. All of these things about Joey lightened the load of the challenges which came along beside them.

We were blessed with a "nice" doctor; a specialist in the issues of bowel problems. He had a heart of gold, a spirit of kindness. It is a major blessing to have a doctor who will take the time to not rush his consultation and sometimes just visit. Encouraging words went very far as motherhood did not come with a manual and it was sometimes very trying with a special needs baby. This doctor was one I looked forward to seeing. He would always bring something new to talk about. One time the doctor would talk about all the wonders of breast milk, another time it would be about nutrition and security issues for babies. As I had gone through so much to nurse Joey and had so many little things happen I soaked up everything the doctor told me. He confirmed that my efforts were not in vain and hard work does bring its rewards. This favorite doctor of Joey's expressed his own joy when things went well. The doctor said he was so pleased that the muscle was right where it was supposed to be and that there were no complications from the surgery and that the healing was right on target. His words were, "How come this baby heals so well?" That was an open door to tell him how I prayed. The doctor nodded in agreement like he knew. I remember the day we left the hospital after that month- long stay, as this special, nice doctor told us; "The Lord had been kind to you in giving you such a willing and loving baby." "Just look at him, all he wants to do is please." I was so touched and I knew in my heart of hearts, way down in there, that I was truly blessed. He must have known Joey was a *special snowflake*. My faith was being built up through what I went through with my baby and I knew that no situation was ever hopeless with God. Even when I felt I had no hope left, I could still hope for hope, as I served a good God and I was and still remain eternally thankful for the short time with Joseph, even with the circumstances being what they were.

Good doctors and determined moms are quite a team to affirm success in babies healing and growing. But Jesus was the hand that did the guiding, comforting, and the ultimate healing. Great doctors, faithful moms, and competent nurses can only do so much. I believe health care workers are all very aware of their limitations as they see so much in the work they do daily. I am sure doctors' abilities are tested a lot as they experience the loss of lives.

My own limits were pushed watching the process of intravenous needles find a vein and then fall out. I hated needles, so when the intravenous needle would keep falling out I'd leave the room and go to my source, God, and pray. The nurse said Joey was really good and did not make a sound. Yes, another little miracle. I knew God showed up or rather was there all along knowing my limitations. God blessed me and Joe again. I could count on God's love.

There was always something new to learn living in a children's hospital ward for a month. Blessings and challenges were a daily happening.

I dreaded the doctor's assignments he gave me. One was the necessary task of dilating Joey's anus opening in order to assist the progress of passing stool. Up until the anus reversal surgery the colostomy was like an automatic stool passer but now Joey had to learn a whole new way of doing it. Joey seemed uncomfortable. I was bit neglectful in my assignment from the doctor and since Joey was passing some stool. I didn't think it was that important. I would learn the hard way when we got home just how important it was to do this simple task.

Our last day at the hospital was nearing and so was Joey's birthday. I was hopeful we would be home in time to celebrate his birthday with family. Instead we were scheduled to leave our hotel hospital on the exact date of Joey's birthday. Joe's birthday present would be another plane ride to go home on. I was happily preparing for our departure when we had one more happy hospital event. Surprisingly, from around the corner came nurses with a beautiful birthday cake and a happy birthday song. That was the one and only birthday cake Joey and I shared, a memory to treasure and it didn't seem to matter we were in hotel hospital. I loved it, as it had white icing with blue icing trim and *Happy Birthday* written on top with one single beautiful blue candle.

We had a party with our special hospital staff, who became our friends.

Travel and exhaustion were on the list for the rest of our day. I was anxious and lonesome for the family at home. That was one time I did not pray for patience and as the saying goes, "haste makes waste" and I forgot an important detail. I forgot to mention to the doctor Joe's discomfort. Joey was still in recovery mode and I could have possibly saved us some trauma. Joey's skin color was off, almost a yellowish tinge; he had dark circles under his eyes, intense gas, and vomiting. I attributed this to what he had been through with the surgery but it continued into the night. Being home was short-lived, as we rushed to the hospital again. In frustration, I had to relay all the information about Joey's surgery to the local hospital doctor and so went Joey's birthday and homecoming. Instead of a break from hospital, we had men in white coats, along with tears in Joey's eyes. The doctors were extremely concerned, I was scared and Joey was probably downright mad. Joey's poor little eyes were white, swollen, puffy, and lifeless looking. It always amazes me how some days are so long and others so short yet both have same number of hours. The night dragged on as we once again explained to the new doctors Joey's ordeal at Children's Hospital. The doctors were focused on Joey's heart rate. The doctors kept saying the heart rate was well over two hundred, sounding like an athlete's running a race. The doctor's lingo caused me even more alarm. Then they put an ice pack on Joey's face and gave him another x-ray. X-rays are not fun, especially when one is tired sick and stressed. They involve stripping Joey of warm clothes, strapping him in and mom stretching his arms high up. Joey had to resign himself to another intravenous and another night in the hotel hospital. Once again, mother was off to the telephone prayer lines.

In the morning I sensed the light of the sunrise shining through a dark cloud. The emergency doctors had done their work and contacted the previous doctors from Children's Hospital. Joey's present problem was severe constipation. Joey required extra help to alleviate the problem, which meant two more days in hospital. Finally, Joey knew how his own bed felt after a memorable birthday and more hospital life. Doctor visits were planned to monitor

Joey's bowel protocol. We were both tired of hospitals and doctors, but we needed them.

Surgeries often are a shock to our bodily functions and come with a risk. If there is no follow-up, things can easily go wrong, as it happened for Joey. I often felt like I was in a school due to the medical professionals being such a major part of Joey's life. Of course, they were an only a small part of my learning; the big part was lessons from God. God is love and I was learning love lessons.

Continual reminders were ever-present, such as that God is all powerful, God brings things to pass according to His timing, God knows the beginning and the end, God is eternal. I live in a natural state with a God who is supernatural. Every step I walk is dependent on "Trusting God," as I discover more of God's truth. In Proverbs 21:24 (Living Bible), it states: **"Since the Lord is directing our steps, why try to understand everything that happens along the way?"**

I loved my snowflake and God's living word.

I read in 2 Corinthians 5:16–18 (New International Version): "Therefore we do not lose heart. Even though our outward man is perishing, yet the inward man is being renewed day by day. For our light affliction, which is but for a moment, is working for a far more exceeding and eternal weight of glory, while we do not look at the things which are seen? For the things which are seen are temporary, but the things which are not seen are eternal."

It is better to depend on an eternal God than my own experiences. My experiences would change, but not God, His promises, or His eternal word. In Isaiah 40:8 I read: "The grass withers, the flower fades, but the word of God stands forever."

God became more and more personal. I never fully understood at the time what God was doing in my life when I had Joey. Now I can say I understand in part. I understand how God created in me a heart for other individuals who are just like my son Joey. If I see a Down syndrome individual in a crowd, I desire to give them a hug. Maybe that is why I worked with two Down syndrome individuals for over twenty years. That was a privilege for me. Joey's life impacted much of what I did for much of my life. What a difference Joey made in my life.

Joey gave life a new meaning of unconditional love. The Lord taught me that His love is unconditional. In the Bible one of the most quoted verses is 1 Corinthians 13:13: "And now abide in faith, hope and love, these three: but the greatest of these is love." Also it goes on to say much about love: "Love suffers long and is kind, love does not envy; love does not parade itself and is not puffed up, does not behave rudely, does not seek its own, is not provoked, thinks no evil, does not rejoice in iniquity, but rejoices in the truth, bears all things, believes all thing, hopes all things, endures all things. Love never fails." I am still learning to understand the true unconditional God kind of love. I believe learning how to love is the most important accomplishment one should obtain in living.

The Bible gives another definition on love in 1 John 4:7: "Dear friends, let us love one another, because love comes from God. Whoever loves is a child of God and knows God. Whoever does not love does not know God, for God is love. He sent his only Son into the world, so that we may have life through Him: this is what love is: it is not that we have loved God, but that He loved us more and sent His Son to be the means which sins are forgiven."

Love is what God is all about and as we walk in God's ways and learn of Him we will be made more into His likeness and His divine love.

Love shined through in my little snowflake.

Chapter 6
Handmaidens with love

THERE WAS AN INSERT IN my Bible that was written by Kathryn Kuhlman that goes as follows: "If you want a simple word to characterize the person of God, all you have to do is take four letters and write them over and over again—the word love—and that is God."

God loves without end, seeks only for our good. The Lord lifts us up as we turn to Him. In James 4:10 it reads: "Humble yourselves (feeling very insignificant) in the presence of the Lord, and He will exalt you (He will lift you up and make your lives significant)."

God's love lifts us up where we belong as His children. This reminds me of the classic song. I wrote part of it below.

"Love lifts us up where we belong"

Who knows what tomorrow brings
In a world where few hearts survive
I know the way I feel

When it's real
I keep it alive

The road is long
There are mountains in the way,
But we climb a step every day

[Chorus]
Love lifts us up where we belong,
Where the eagles fly
On a mountain high
Love lift us up where we belong

(Written by Jack Nitzsche, Buffy Sainte-Marie, and
Will Jennings)Recorded by Joe Cocker)

Walking in God's love is real as we follow Christ and enter in through Jesus, who is the way. From 1 Corinthians 13 I quote: "I may be able to speak the languages of men and even angels, but if I have no love, my speech is no more than a noisy gong or a clanging bell. I may have the gift of inspired preaching, I may have all the knowledge and understand, all secrets, I may have all the faith needed to move mountains—but if I have no love, I am nothing."

Today I can only see part of the knowledge and wisdom of God's knowledge and power. Yet like the wind, I know when it's there. I like to quote here 1 Corinthians 13:11: "When I was a child, my speech, feelings and thinking were all of those of a child; now that I am a man, I have no more use for childish ways. What we see now is like a dim image in a mirror; then we shall see face to face. What I know now is only partial; then it will be complete as God's knowledge of me."

Obviously, we are to grow in the things of God continually. Like the saying goes, "There is a God and I am not Him."

I am glad, for the Bible teaches me in Romans 8:39: "Nor height, nor depth, nor any other creature, shall be able to separate us from the love of God, which is in Christ Jesus our Lord."

The sweetness and preciousness of unconditional love God poured out for both Joey and me. God loved me and I was given the privilege of knowing the greatness of a divine love through a Down syndrome baby, a snowflake. It was a divine honor in an appointed time in my life. I cannot completely express the special love I experienced. Walking with God through valleys is an honor. God can use just a little snowflake to do great work and change in one's heart and life. It would be a shame to clone a snowflake when all have a unique purpose. I need to give honor to God throughout Joey's book, as He is the divine Heavenly Father who lives in and through me, and gave me the blessed privilege to know Joe.

God is my loving Father and my desire is to be more like Him. I believe my cup overflows in His love. I read a poem once from a church bulletin that speaks on perfect love. It is as follows.

"Perfect Love Is"

Slow to suspect
Quick to trust
Slow to condemn
Quick to justify
Slow to offend
Quick to defend
Slow to expose
Quick to shield
Slow to belittle
Quick to appreciate
Slow to demand
Quick to give
Slow to provoke

Quick to win over
Slow to hinder
Quick to help
Slow to resentment
Quick to forgive

To walk in that kind of perfect love would take a lot more of God and a lot less of us. Perfect love puts others best interests first, appreciating our strengths and helping our brothers in their weaknesses. We should aim to grow in perfect love for one another. God honors and helps us in our walk towards it.

The Bible says! John 4:18(King James Version)"There is no fear in love; but perfect love casteth out fear because fear hath torment. He that feareth is not made perfect in love."

God is perfect love and we need to be free from fear to become complete in love. God's love will cast out fear.

More of 1 John 4:19–21 says, "We love Him because He first loved us. If a man says I love God, and hates his brother, he is a liar, for he that loves not his brother whom he hath seen, how can he love God whom he has not seen. And these commandments have we from Him, that he who loves God loves his brother also."

My handmaidens were to me Gods secret agents. I never knew when they would show up!

(Thessalonians 5; 11) ;(New International version)"Therefore encourage one another and build each other up, just as in fact you are doing."

A sister in the Lord sent me an encouraging letter, included below:

Dear Becky,

I was saddened to hear of the health of your son. I am sure it will work out for the best. The Bible tells us we are given children that God chooses for us especially. You have a great capacity for love, and children with Down syndrome are the most loving people one could have. Perhaps also God feels you all need the purity of innocent love this child can give you. Believe me, it is quite an experience to be loved totally without reservation. Being loved this way can be a healing experience for everyone around. The one thing I would like to stress is the love part because we all need to be loved and cared for without any reservations. We tend to say I love that person because—and we stipulate why. However, this does not have to be so. We can love each other no matter how we dislike what others say or do. I wish for you and your son, love.

The kind of love mentioned in the letter comes with no strings attached, a wonderful, pure love. When I look over the letter it sounds like a prophecy that I experienced with Joe. I know Jesus loved me through Joey's trails and challenges.

I received another letter from a handmaiden of the Lord. It is as follows:

Dear Becky,

I thought I'd take the time just to let you know I am thinking about you and not really sure what to say to you so I will just let it come from the heart. I know you believe in prayers, so I am praying for you, and I too believe in them. Life sure can be confusing at times, can't it? I guess growing older makes you realize just how unpredictable life can be. Sometimes we kind of have to sit back and let things happen as they unfold. It can be so hard at times but you know

> Becky, it always turns out in the end, there's always something good or special to be gained from those times. Love you.

Little did my friend know how much good and specialness came because Joey was born. I had a friend who took the time to give love in words of encouragement. No one should ever think twice about sending a note to encourage someone, even if they feel they lack the right words. People need to know that others care and support them. The receiver may be like me and latch on the heart of a letter for so long it ends up in a book. Also, kindness is catchy; the more one does the more others do.

Another letter that confirms much of what I have talked about throughout Joey's story was from a sister in the Lord. Kindness and love flowed through her words. I unfortunately do not remember the sister's name. The letter is as follows:

> Dear Becky,
>
> Just a few words to let you know our heartfelt love goes out to you at this time. We sympathize because of the anguish you have already gone through and because we love you. We know the many shed and not yet shed tears that have been part of and will be part of your life. We had a baby who was mentally challenged at one time who later died of crib death. For years I was tortured by the thought that there must have been something I could have done, even after the doctors and nurses told me nothing could have been done. However, I often think of what that little spirit did for me. First of all, I think the little spirit who was sent or offered to come down filled the needs in that wee body. Through the rest of my

lifetime I have been able to comfort and help those who have had the same experience, for I know the searching that I went through. So the spirit in your little boy's body will do what it was sent to do and you will become even more loving, more caring, and more sympathetic towards others with problems of the same sort. It's funny in a way that the proud human race often looks down in disdain at its failures, its cripples, its old and senile, its blind and deaf mutes and cannot relate to them in any way until they have been touched personally by those same defects. Even then many cannot accept these things. (As you know I felt and sensed this often). How hard it must be for those people to meet the master who said, "I was sick and in prison and you visited me not, I was hungered and ye gave me no meat I was thirsty and ye gave me no drink. Depart from me ye cursed into everlasting fire" (Matt. 25:36–47). I got it backwards but it's all in there. I am not talking about you, because you are very loving and caring but somewhere along the line others have and will be touched and you will never be the same again because of this small baby. I also want you to know that our family and church members are praying for you and if you relax and leave things in Christ's hands you will feel a peacefulness fall over you that deny understanding.

The sister had her own little snowflake too. The lady was right about what a *difference* Joey would make in my life. I had friends who supported me with their whole heart and soul. I would do what she said and often put everything in God's hands and His peace would come. I can sincerely say God surely used women of God to bring comfort and I hope God's love will touch many through letters I have passed on here in Joey's story.

Some readers have their own story but have yet to come into God's healing and saving grace, or even to come to a place of accepting a handicapped child. To come to a place where God's love surrounds and fills one's being is to be in a place where life and hope lives. It is the place of ultimate love that last forever with God. Joey's story is all about love. God's love is like a magnet and many are drawn to it in this world as they search for love in other temporal things, things that don't satisfy. In the world today, we know about love and have all the types of love, such as friendship love, which is often based on feelings and says, "If you love me I will love you back." This is a selfish type of love and not what God intended for us. God's love sticks closer than a friend. Then there is the natural love within families that says, "You're my family, my brother, so I will love you," but even that love can fail for selfish reasons. Sometimes family love is sincere, but all I am saying is it can be subject to failure as it needs the spiritual foundation of God's love to last.

God's love does not fail. The greatest gift of all is God's perfect love. John 15:13 says: "Greater love has no one than this, than to lay down one's life for his friends." And that is what Jesus did for mankind on the cross. Jesus is the way, the truth and the light. Jesus loves naturally, supernaturally and perfectly. Gods loves us, never forsakes us, and desires to be our friend.

I think much of the problems in life stem from loneliness. It can almost feel like a disease when we feel very alone. One needs to know that when times come into our lives and friends leave or fail us for whatever reason, God can send some new friends, often just when we think no one cares. God is always there for us even when we reach rock-bottom despair we have a true friend in Jesus. I have experienced the loss of a good friend only to have new friendships appear. I knew God was behind it. God has sent many spirit-filled women walking in His ways to do His will. I call them his handmaidens.

When one has a defining moment in life, such as a nurse saying, "You had a baby boy and he has Down syndrome," it can be not only a defining moment but also a dark moment. Fears try to grab at your very being. How will I care for him? What will his life be like? Will people accept him? To have and know you have supporting friends in both deed and prayer is a lifeboat. When the valley is at its very darkest moment and you know God is holding your hand you can get through and over it all.

I wonder how God could love me and care so much for me that if I had been the only one to have lived He would have died for me. How can it be possible? God is pure, righteous, and holy yet still loves and values me and does not make junk. Therefore, I cannot criticize myself, as I am God's handiwork. I will choose to love myself so I can love God and others. The golden rule says "that I do unto others as I would want them to do unto me." How can I do well and love others if I did not even love myself?

Love never ends. I had a taste of God's perfect love in and though a baby boy with Down syndrome, truly a gift from God. I find it hard to believe that in some countries having a special needs child is actually considered a curse. Apparently in some places they leave handicapped children to fend for themselves and often are ignored. This is heartbreaking in every sense of the word. An encounter with God would shine the light on the value of all human life.

I am very thankful for the wonderful love relationship with my baby, Joseph John. I am thankful God never let go of my hand. There were times I let go of God's hand and lived to regret it. I am thankful God still heard my prayers and helped me get back where I knew I should be. By not quitting I became stronger. God's hand gave me safety and assurance that I could not find anywhere else.

Handmaidens of God helped me see the light and helped carry my load. It is tough to have to go through the trials of any sick baby let alone one with life-threatening complications. God sends help through His handmaidens and all sorts of life boats because he is a good God, a good father and wants me happy. I had to learn God's purpose for me was to put Him first in all things and to be above all my first love. I knew what His word said in 2 Corinthians 11–12: "For I am a jealous God for you with a Godly jealousy." And in Exodus 20:5, when God was talking about false gods and said, "You shall not bow down to them, For I the Lord your God am a jealous God."

In God's classroom—with a Down syndrome baby and all the hurdles of learning new things for him, such as nursing, colostomy care, physiotherapy classes, and heart issues—I remained eternally thankful for all of God's spirit-filled handmaidens.

God's wish for my best came through when I looked upon Joey and his perfect smile. I saw and experienced a perfect love. *My perfect little snowflake!*

Chapter 7
Parenting Joey and his siblings

JOEY'S OLDER BROTHER DARREN WAS eight years of age and full of questions. I always told Darren how perfect Joey was and to never to worry what anyone may say about him and that the most important thing in the world was love. It's our differences that make us all special. Darren was a sensitive boy and seemed to understand. I would just point out Joey's beautiful smile and the picture was worth a thousand words. Joey's undeniable love spoke volumes to us all.

I said, "Darren, take a real good long look and you will see how Joey always returns your attention to him with a huge smile." I said, "Darren, think about how Joey just loves us and enjoys just being with us. We are so blessed to have him. Joey is a happy and joyful little person."

Darren was accepting and loved his baby brother as any brother would. I often felt I had to counsel those in Joey's life and found myself going on about different truths such as, "If we had all the gold in the world but no one to share it with what good would it do? If you had all the beautiful clothes money could buy but no one to wear them and compliment you what would it mean? If you had the most beautiful house in the world to live in but no one loved you and you had no one to share it with what kind of home would it be?" I would also say, "Darren, stop and look at Joey, why he doesn't even know yet about a house, clothes, or money. All he knows is us and love so really we are learning from him about what matters in life. We all know money helps but it cannot buy happiness."

My conversations were positive with Joey's siblings. "Happy" was Joey's middle name when he was at home with family close. We would catch him copying what he saw us do. I'd praise all my children so that we could enjoy the little things more knowing full-well the small things would contribute in a big way to Joey's abilities and future. And it all came easily in our home environment because of the fun that came with enjoying Joey's nature and personality.

The Bible says, "Never despise small beginnings", we never took anything for granted.

Joey's whole heart was on his sleeve when he was just doing small things like banging a pot during his physiotherapy routine. Joey would glance up as if to say, "Hey, did you see that?" So many seemingly unimportant things brought laughter and lightened the ever-present thought that Joey was handicapped. We would all cheer Joey on when he would clap his tiny hands together and try his hardest to stack toy red blocks. We would all giggle as it was so obvious how Joey enjoyed himself during planned therapy activities. The teacher, his family, and I cheered for Joey with gusto, especially since we knew Joey had the tendency to get tired quickly due to his tiny heart with the quarter-sized hole in the middle of it. Joey would often sleep for long periods but more so after activities. We all did our best as Joe's health issues loomed over us.

I knew it was a serious responsibility to teach those closest to Joey how to treat others and discover the things that count in life.

I know I would have made every day exceptional if I had known how short his life was going to be. Enjoyment would have been the focus of Joey's life instead of questioning what the future would hold for him. I wanted a strong support for Joey and I thought the path had to be paved all the way from birth. I felt I had a job to guide and develop others to support Joey. This was all good as long as my focus was to live in the present.

To be a positive influence as a parent is essential. I wanted my children to be leaders and remember to never look down upon those who seem different .It could have been one of us born with an extra chromosome. God is interested in molding character in such a way that children will grow to see and experience the goodness of God. God develops us all from the inside out. The potter is Jesus and we are the clay. Matthew 5:7 says, "Blessed are the meek; for they shall inherit the earth." In Hebrew the translation of meek means to be molded, Psalm 37:11 says, "But the meek shall inherit the earth, and shall delight themselves in the abundance of peace." To be molded into God's image brings one peace. This was and is my desire for my children throughout the entirety of their lives. All children are a gift from God and he can and does use them to teach parents about His love and to mold our character. Raising children really is twofold. Parents learns as they help children grow and sometimes it means parents need to first grow up and possibly in a hurry. There are many books on parenting but the greatest wisdom is still the Bible.

Parents have a grave responsibility that brings both heartache and rewards. We can never underestimate the job of parenting. We influence our children in both the naturally and spiritually, they are our future. We need to remember that our children believe whatever we tell them.

Praise a child and watch him bloom. The Bible says, Proverbs 23; 7 "For as a man thinks in his heart, so is he, "When we speak good things to our children they will think good of themselves.

We must always plant good seeds (words), as it is God's principle that we will reap what we sow .James 3; 13; says, "Who is there among you who is wise and intelligent? Then let him by his noble living show forth his (good) works with the (unobtrusive) humility (which is the proper attribute) of true wisdom." Obviously, our words are to be chosen with wisdom as words have the power to build up or tear down.

As a young mother I had much to learn and mistakes were made, but love covers never fails. Loving children is the glue for teaching and guiding.

One time I was feeling low as a single mom and complained to God about how I had no job and I sensed the Lord, whisper, "Yes you do, your job is your children."

The following article is meant to encourage. I was encouraged in parenting Joey and his siblings with the message.

"Beatitudes for Parents"

Blessed are the parents who make their peace with spilled milk and mud, for of such is the kingdom of childhood.

Blessed is the parent who engages not in the comparison of his child with others, for precious unto each is the rhythm of his own growth.

Blessed are the fathers and mothers who have learned laughter, for it is the music of the child's world.

Blessed and wise are those parents who understand the goodness of time, for they make it not a sword that kills growth, but a shield to protect.

Blessed and mature are they who without anger can say "no," for comforting to the child is the security of firm decisions.

Blessed is the gift of consistency, for it is heart's ease in childhood.

Blessed are they who accept the awkwardness of growth, for they are aware of the constant perilous choice between marred furnishings and damaged personalities.

Blessed are the teachable, for knowledge brings understanding, and understanding brings love.

Blessed are the men and women who, in the midst of the uncompromising mundane, give love, for they bestow the greatest of all gifts-to each other, to their children, and in an ever-widening circle, to their fellow men.

(Marion Kinneman)

I think one can conclude that being the best role model we can will have far-reaching effects on raising children. Children seem to see better then they hear.

Proverbs 22:6: "Train up a child the way he should go and he will not depart from it." Knowing and following through is what counts.

One thing I know for sure is that Joseph's love taught us to value life and its fragility. I learned quickly that all children are different and having a disability doesn't mean less than lovable, but can mean quite the opposite—more than lovable. Given fair chances many reach their full potential. When supported physically, emotionally, and spiritually we can exceed all preconceived expectations. Loving and supporting those most in need is God's love in action.

"All we need is love" is true if we do more living it and less talking about it. As the old saying goes, "I'd rather see a sermon than hear one any day."

Now we live more in the age of "what is online?" We can even find anything about parenting online. The good thing is we can find the old-fashioned Bible, which does not fail online. The Bible covers it all for living, teaching, and love.

What a change we would see in the world if we could all have a heart furnished with humility, and be truthful in love and expectant of God's leading, and just love those not easily accepted into society.

Don't clone a snowflake!

Our children can be the greatest teachers about humility. What is humility? I think it may be accepting that we never know it all. The opposite of humility is thinking one does know it all, which allows in the deadly spirit of pride.

I was humbled with the birth of a handicapped child and felt totally at the mercy of God, as time passed I discovered how little I knew. I suddenly had a whole new world to explore.

I often found myself watching Joey as he slept and pondering the mysteries of life. I loved to watch Joey sleep as it was a peaceful quiet time and he seemed to employ the presence of Almighty God. I also felt sleep was a precious time for Joey too. He had pain and precious sleep would bring relief. How could Joey's naps bring such peace and a golden silence? I knew this baby would make a real difference in my life forever. I would grow, see more clearly, love more dearly, accept more readily, and put off things that counted for nothing and concentrate on those things that were worth mentioning.

Joey and his siblings are three special gifts and I love all three equally. It didn't matter if one had an extra chromosome or one had blue eyes or if the other was blonde. I was a parent who loved parenting and they remain snowflakes, unique and special. I am shocked that some countries have a law to force parents to abort because a baby has an extra chromosome. I believe it is very dangerous ground to walk on when laws take over God's job.

I am reminded of a story I wanted to tell my other children when they got older. It goes like this. One day I was on the bus and a man named Steve introduced himself to me. I immediately thought, "Wow, this guy is happy about something." He was obviously anxious to have a conversation and didn't seem important who he conversed with as long as they would lend an ear. After a minute or two I realized this Steve was "slow," appearing to have Down syndrome. For someone "slow," he was happy and in a hurry to meet and talk to someone. Stranger or not, it did not matter to Steve. I was bored so it was pleasing to have someone to chat with on the bus ride. Most other passengers would glance away and not acknowledge Steve or me but I never cared. It was a great and awesome experience to talk to someone who was so happy. It was great to not think about my worries and what I had to do today but instead enjoy someone who only wanted a listening ear. Steve went on about how grateful he was to have a job. I was dreading going to mine today. What a revelation. I should be more thankful, someone else would be really happy to have my job. Steve went on to talk about his strike at the bowling alley and his sick friend he would see tonight who might go to heaven. Suddenly, I realized life is short, and I wished I appreciated it more, no longer wanting to be unemployed, unfriendly, or forgetful of my friends. I saw past the Down syndrome and saw the wonderful man who gave me a gift of thankfulness.

It was an awesome bus ride!

Having a sure foundation in God's word is like a blind man who has a cane. The blind man cannot see where he's going but give him a cane and he can get about and that's one way of explaining how it works by having God's word in hand; He will be our guide.

God's will is that all receive salvation, the gospel message, and eternal life in heaven. By receiving Christ into one's heart we have invited in a best friend who stays forever. The bible states that angels in heaven rejoice over the salvation of even one soul. In God's world miracles and healing are naturally supernatural.

Sometimes one needs an inner miracle in their soul, not always a physical healing, as our bodies are temporal and our souls are eternal. All us believers get new bodies in heaven but our souls are forever and every man decides which way his soul will go by accepting or rejecting Jesus.

Palms 41:4; reads: "Lord be merciful to me and heal my soul." This made me wonder what happens to one's soul when heartbreak happens. Often times healing in the body happens after an inner soul healing; for example, being delivered from unforgiveness. Only God knows what needs healing, as he sees the motives of the heart or soul man. God works in the supernatural and always has a plan and His plan is good.

Joey's life had a plan. Joey was pure and whole in the eyes of God and was about his Father's business. Joe's soul was perfect. Joey's body needed healing. I believe baby Joey with Down syndrome made a *difference* in my soul.

God gave me dreams. In this one dream I saw all these special need individuals singing and worshipping God at a school and the teacher in charge said, "Someone please stop them." I answered with, "You try." It opened my eyes knowing that their spirit was pure and it welcomed the Holy Spirit by worshipping. It was a defining dream.

My greatest love-walk with Jesus was when Joey was with me and his health issues loomed over me daily. The Bible says: "God is our refuge and strength, an ever present help in times of trouble" (Psalm 46:1). God helped strengthen me to be a parent of three children even through health issues. Sometimes all three children were sick at same time.

One of my favorite songs is "All Is Well with My Soul." Apparently the writer (Horatio Spafford) of the song wrote the words to this song during what had to be the most trying times of his life. He had lost his real estate to Chicago fires and so sent his family ahead of him to start a new life in a new country, but on the way he lost four daughters in a ship wreck. The writer went to the very spot where the daughters died and he wrote the song, "All Is Well with My Soul." That had to be a very dark moment, yet he still trusted God.

The following is an excerpt on one person's interpretation on 1 Corinthians 13. The writer interestingly called it: "A Self-Concept on the Process to Change."

"A Self-Concept on the Process to Change."

Because God loves me, He is slow to lose patience with me.

Because God loves me He takes the circumstances of my life and uses them in a constructive way for my growth.

Because God loves me He does not treat me like an object to be possessed and manipulated.

Because God loves me He has no need to impress me with how great and powerful He is because He is God, nor does He belittle me as His child in order to show me how important He is.

Because God loves me He is for me, He wants to see me grow and develop in His love.

Because God loves me He does not send down His wrath on every little mistake I make, of which there are many.

Because God loves me He doesn't keep score of all my sins then beat me over the head whenever He gets the chance.

Love forgets mistakes.

Because God loves me He is grieved when I do not walk in the ways that please Him because He sees this as evidence that I don't trust and love Him as I should.

Because God loves me He rejoices when I experience His power and strength and I stand up under pressures.

Because God loves me He keeps on working patiently with me when I feel like giving up and I can't see why He doesn't give up on me.

Because God loves me He never says there is not hope for me, rather He works patiently with me, loves me, disciplines me in such a way it is hard for me to understand His dept of concern for me.

God is the perfect Father and with God leading, parenting is adventure.

The interpretation of Corinthians 13 is the *love* chapter in the Bible.

Chapter 8
Heart surgery Looms

THE OPERATION FOR COLOSTOMY REVERSAL allowed for three months of freedom from colostomy bags. Joey rolled and played on his tummy with glee. And I'll never forget the powerhouse Joey became at bath time. We enjoyed each other, my little snowflake and I. But heart surgery was a stretch for me. I had to lean into God's wisdom, His spirit, His power and not man's. I had to stand in faith that God had a plan regarding Joey's heart surgery. This was a major surgery for Joe and a major test for me. I needed to trust God.

With a thankful heart I repeated my theme song, "*God is a Good God.*" Heart surgery for baby Joey meant counting my blessings, it was a miracle Joey lived at birth. Scriptures like Isaiah 26:3 came into my mind: "Thou will keep him in perfect peace whose mind is stayed on thee." And the word worked for me. As Bible says, "God's word does not come back void." I trusted Jesus to be with Joe.

I have to be real. I was nervous. But God the eternal Father was more real than my nervousness; God showed up in the little things, so why not the big ones?

As a baby Christian at that time, I had lots of growing to do. I had lots to learn. I would read one verse and repeat it to carry me through. One word of God is powerful, Hebrews 4:12: "For the word of God is powerful, and sharper than any two-edged sword, piercing even to the dividing of the joints and marrow, and is a discerner of the thoughts and intents of the heart."

With Joey and the trauma of heart surgery, the power of God's word gave me hope.

Being thankful kept me from becoming bitter and allowed the memories to be joyous!

1 Thessalonian 5:12 says, "Rejoice always, pray without ceasing, and in everything give thanks; for this is the will of God in Christ Jesus for you." I believe the Bible verse is referring to one's attitude and I need to be responsible in my thinking. Blessings and good was always the side effects of responsible choices.

In life's unfairness I have a traveling companion, my Lord who honored me with a baby named Joey for a short season of my life. The maturity came in my soul just like a tiny tree in a forest of larger oak trees. The mighty oak was once a tiny tree like me and had to grow, mostly in storms.

I became a student when Joey was born. I had much to learn. I know a valley can be one of the highest peaks in life. I was in a valley of *how's* and *whys* but God was my source.

I certainly had to exercise humility. The word of God says in James 4:6, "God resists the proud but gives grace to the humble." I don't know if I was humble but I was humbled when heart surgery was looming. God's grace carried me through. I was blessed with the presence of the Holy Spirit. God was my anchor and he would get me through the storms. With trust came the peace.

A secret to getting through so many life challenges, such as a handicapped child, is to drop all the *whys*, all *what's* and *how's*, and accept God knows as sometimes we may never know.

God gives me the knowledge that it's not all about me but instead what God's plan is for me.

God could heal Joey instantly or decide to have me grow in the journey. God held our future in His hands. I knew I committed Joey to God when baby Joey was in my womb. Trusting was not an option.

Before heart surgery Joey had prep-heart surgery. I recall my mind playing tricks on me sometimes. I would see something like a flash card in my mind that read, "heart surgery." Even then, God brought peace. In quietness and confidence, I received God's strength. In the silence I could hear peace be still. How can we hear God's voice at all in this noisy world? Maybe that's why we dream.

God spoke to me many times in dreams. One time I had a dream about seven parables. In each of these parables I had a sense that said "God does the impossible." The one that stood out the most in the dream was the last parable of the seven. In this one I saw scenery, the same scenery I see out my kitchen window when awake. This scenery was of the hills, trees, power lines, and rooftops. I looked away for only a minute and upon looking back out the window the scenery changed completely. I was stunned and thought to myself how quickly things can change. The scenery was much more beautiful. The ordinary hills were suddenly snow-capped and no longer hills but mountainous, and the farther I looked into the distance the more beautiful they became. The view took on a spiritual, heavenly-like beauty, none I have lived to see on earth. I became quite excited when watching this scene in my dream and turned to call my sister to the window to share it with her. She exclaimed, "That's so beautiful." I answered her with, "Yes, more beautiful than we could have ever imagined," adding", now isn't that just like God, to be able to turn something so ordinary into something so extraordinarily beautiful. "I know that I could move those mountains through faith in the power of God." I also said, "I saw those mountains start to actually move." I believe this was a word from God to help me see His majesty and power and grow in my faith. To also know what I see is not always what God sees, as he sees in the supernatural and I see in the natural. This dream was now a long time ago, but I can still remember it very clearly. It was a spoken word from God in a dream and Gods word lives forever.

Romans 8:7 says, "We are more than conquers through Him that loved us" and Matthew 17:20 says, "If you have faith as a mustard seed, you will be able to say to this mountain, move from here to there, and it will move: and nothing shall be impossible for you." Simply put, I was learning "lots."

What a *difference* Joey made in my life. Just one little snowflake!

I chose to have faith and trust God for baby Joseph to be healed. It was easier than going it on my own, to deal with my imagination regarding the looming surgeries. In faith I believed completely; Joey would become whole physically. Yet just like my dream, I did not at first see the whole picture. God was both preparing me and shielding me.

I knew Joey was whole and perfect needing only healing physically. God made Joseph and he would take care of my baby. Surgery and trauma would both pass. I would get through it. I had to believe to receive from the Lord's hand. Trusting God was a safe spot to be. I looked up to where my help came from, Jesus.

Pre-surgeries and heart surgery spell stress for both the mom and patient. I often thought to myself that it would be helpful to have a visible sign in children's wards that read, "When you are looking at a sick child there is usually a stressed parent close by. Pray for both."

I recall one of my quiet days when I was off alone with my thoughts. It was one of those serene days when heaven felt close by. I was about to lay Joey down for his regular afternoon nap after a refreshing bath. The smell of a baby all freshened up is cuddly stuff for mom and baby. In the quietness, I felt like I could hear a peaceful silence. As I laid Joey into his crib I shook his toy mobile to give him a distraction when I left the room, but this day was different. Joey just refused to take his eyes off of me. I thought I must get to my household chores but as I got only to the doorway of his room I felt a need to stop and listen. I heard a still, small voice say, "Life is short, go back and spent some more time." So I went back to Joey's bedside and noticed that he was staring off into what looked like the corner of the ceiling.

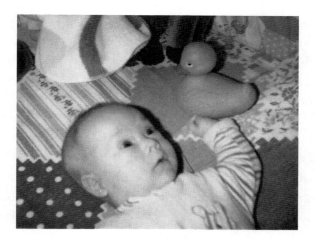

I started a conversation with my baby, saying, "Joey, do you see angels up there?" Joey heard my voice and stared again into my eyes. I saw those "Jesus eyes" and I sensed Joey was listening closely to my every word so I continued to talk away, saying, "Joey you are so beautiful and Momma loves you so very much and I want you to know we still have a lot to go through. Your heart surgery is coming up soon, so don't you dare die on me as I will not forgive you and will be very, very sad. I love you so much Joey." (Of course I never was unforgiving about Joey dying.) I was just babbling on till I noticed a tear trickle down his check, without him making any sounds. It was not without a special sense of peace in between us, the special peace that only comes from Jesus. I responded by picking Joey up and hugging him, saying, "Joey you don't know what I said, now you stop that." I laid him back down for a nap and went on with my everyday chores, yet that day remains another defining moment for me and my Joey. When I look back on it I believe Joey knew in his spirit the whole time what the future would be for us and he communed with Jesus. Kind of like Joey just knew he had a short time with me and a divine purpose in making a *difference* in my life. I remember often making remarks like, "Joey just knows stuff and understands what I say." Of course he was a baby, not talking yet, and had Down syndrome, so how could that be? But I had special communication so that was good enough for me. Heart surgery was just around the corner so every moment in time counted.

Another special memory about Joey involved a visit from a therapist, who remarked that Down syndrome children often play in cupboards before they crawl or sit. I thought, Okay I'll watch for it, and sure enough, the very next chance Joey got; he was off playing in cupboards as if to say, "I heard that." Joe sure enjoyed banging those pots and pans as loud as possible. I think Joe takes after me, as I enjoy banging pots too, on New-year's eve!

Joey was a social butterfly, always loving company and atten-tion. Every chance he got he would be pulling on someone's shirt sleeve or making his way close to his siblings. Joey had no problem getting where he wanted to go. When he heard his siblings playing in another room he scooted off to the sound of their voices, as if he was saying, "Wait for me. I want to be where all the action is." Special memories are tucked in a special place in my heart, whereby his special needs doesn't even matter. Joey didn't let his heart condition slow him down when he wanted interaction with his siblings. Joey was a family guy.

Don't clone a snowflake!

I hold dear my special memories just like this gospel Hymn (credited to J.B.F. Wright in 1925)

"Precious Memories"

Precious memories, how they linger
How they ever flood my soul,
In the stillness, of the midnight
Precious, sacred scenes unfold
Precious memories, unseen angels
Sent from somewhere to my soul
How they linger, ever near me
And the sacred past unfold.
Precious father, loving mother (loving Joey)
Fly across the lonely years:
And old home scenes of (Joe's) short life
In fond memories appear

I changed the lines a bit for sake of Joe's story. I think back on how I would often catch Joey staring at his siblings and I would have to wonder, "Looks like Joey is taking in it all, like a sunset about to go down, taking in a very last look."

Yes, the Lord was tugging at my heart, preparing me for the inevitable and I wondered did Joey know too, in his spirit?

I recall one Sunday a preacher saying, "If I was going to write a book it would be called 'Why, why, why.'" I surely had a lot of "whys," but God says His word is a lamp unto my feet, thus I believe it's best to forget the *whys* and just trust God. We may never know the *whys* in our lifetime. God, who loves us with ultimate love, will help us through the *whys* and that may be all we need to know.

I don't have all the answers but it's okay because I know the one who does. I never blamed God—He allowed me to have Joey in the first place. Joey was God's before he was mine and where Joey is now is where I'm going too, one fine day!

I was and remain forever blessed!

Before heart surgery I couldn't quite shrug off uneasiness in my spirit.

I've noticed that often before a storm in life, such as death of a loved one, the closest to the lost ones sometimes have a pre-monition of some kind. I had this happen off and on throughout Joey's life but my mindset said otherwise. In my heart somewhere I sensed Joey would not be with me long but my mind firmly went into denial.

One day when Joey's father was carrying him around the house, I noticed how Joey's lungs sounded strangely loud. I said to myself, "I'm sure Joey has a bit of the flu." Little did I know that Joey's lungs were filling with fluid. After Joey's passing, the doctors told me that Joey's lungs were full of fluid and had he lived after the heart surgery, chances were great he would have suffered a lot of pain before dying. His lungs had severe damage by time of heart surgery.

Another time I experienced a flashing red light that said to me in still, small voice, funeral. When this happened I sensed God's presence. I settled it in my mind that my mother would soon be going to heaven as she was aging; little did I know she would outlive my baby, Joey. Despite all the sign posts and red lights I had the faithful friend of denial. Denial stayed close right up the day of Joey's departure to heaven. Sometimes I think maybe denial can be a God-given shield to protect ourselves from what is real. I am convinced the Lord was preparing me all along for Joey's passing just as He did for his birth. Yet not for even a moment did I want to accept Joey would leave me so soon.

The Lord gave insight to my close friend. This particular friend was one of those who come along once in a lifetime, who loved the Lord and loved people. Without God's handmaidens and special agents I would not be where I am today. They all went the extra mile to support me. During the month prior to Joe's heart surgery my friend called several times to tell me to do pictures up of Joey. Her persistence paid off as she finally said she would do it herself if I didn't. I packed up my three children and had a memorable day. All three were happy and co-operative children posing like angels and the pictures couldn't have turned out better. I never saw these pictures till after Joey's heart surgery and death. The timing was amazing.

Joey had sat up so perfect, straight and tall, just as if he knew this would be the "big one," his graduation picture and it turned out to be so. Within the month Joey graduated to his heavenly home. Joey's work was done here on earth. I was never to be the same always looking forward to my own heavenly home-coming. I had a beautiful picture to show off on the cover of Joe's book. We all loved the pictures and showed them off at every opportunity. I think to myself, "Don't Clone a Snowflake."

Family and friends knew in their spirit that Joey's stay would be short. My brother brought my mother for a visit when Joey was a newborn. I was elated and thankful. Visits were rare as my mother lived quite a distance away. What a thrill to have my mother meet my baby, her grandson. I was sure it would be her only visitation as she would not live long. That's what I believed at the time. My beliefs were all backwards.

I was intent on showing my mother how special and beautiful Joey was. I was totally unaware of how much she already knew—she knew this was her one visit with Joey on earth. It was a divine meeting, a very special time between a grandson and a grandmother. During this visit I began my usual normal preaching only this time to my dear mother. I shared about how I felt Joey was a blessing despite his health challenges and about how I had prayed she and Joey would meet. As I talked on I noticed my mother occasionally wipe a tear from her eye. I was touched by my mother's understanding and compassion. I had no idea at that moment what was actually going on. My mom knew Joey would be going home soon to be with Jesus. No wonder tears were in my mother's eyes. It must have been a heart-rending moment for my mother to hold her grandson and know he would soon be leaving and what her daughter would have to endure as a result. I recall her having a hard time looking at baby Joey while I comforted her, saying, "Its okay, he's just fine."

How swift time has flown since those many years ago. Now they are both home. Grandmas and grandchildren must have a blast in heaven.

While my brother and mother were staying at my home, I gave my brother the small book "Angels Unawares" to read. He read it in one night. The next day my brother, Russ, came to me and sat closely beside me. Russ had a strange look on his face, kind of a bewildered look. It was obvious he had something on his mind. So I asked, "What is it?" Russ replied in a quiet, solemn sort of way, "Joey doesn't have a hole in his heart, does he?" I quickly went into explaining the details of Joey's condition and added not to worry, that what happened in the book I gave him (the child died) would never happened to Joey. I explain that it was serious, but medical science could fix defects of the heart. Brother Russ listened intently, yet with a faraway look in his eyes. I look back thinking that while reading the book, the Lord shared something to my brother. The Lord was preparing my family, too. The conversation was encouraging though as Russ lightened up and picked Joseph up into his arms, remarking to us all, "We just might all have ourselves a little angel in our midst." What a joy to have my family understand and support me and know that they too believed what a special blessing Joey really was. Many times I have to wonder, "What is an angel anyway?" and I always think the same answer: Joey was an angel to me!!

Don't Clone a Snowflake.

It's amazing how a mother bear rises up within a mother when it comes to protecting her children. I had a mission to let others know Joey was special, my snowflake. I refused to let others feel sorry for me. I loved opportunities to share Joey's love. I knew Joey's physical health was serious but as far as Down syndrome goes it was just a simple matter of an extra chromosome. I thought the world needed a bit of waking up and I still do. I was not in denial that Joey would need help in life due to Down syndrome but who doesn't? Everyone needs help of some kind. Even had I known about Joe's condition, during my pregnancy abortion would not have even entered my mind *Who aborts a snowflake?*

I continued my mission, letting friends, family, doctors, children, and anyone within earshot in on my walk. I let them know I was blessed and Joseph was perfect. Strangers got to hear my story if they gave me a chance as it came naturally. I was able to spark an interest. One time at a meeting, the topic of discussion was children and support for parenting. I was nervous to speak in front of a group but the Lord tugged my heart and they got an earful about my love for my Down syndrome baby. I choked back tears as I shared Jesus, love, purity, grace, and coming to know the goodness of God through a baby with Down syndrome. God had the podium that day. I shared with joy what a mother with a handicapped child may live with and God's faithfulness. Heart surgery loomed but oh what a journey I was on.

Heart surgery is a risk, a big one, bigger than I imagined. Below is an article that I discovered in my keepsake box. It is about risks.

> To laugh is to risk appearing the fool.
> To weep is to risk appearing sentimental.
> To reach out is to risk involvement.
> To expose feelings is to risk exposing your true self.
> To place your ideas and dreams before the crowd is
> to risk their love.

To love is to risk being loved in return.
To live is to risk dying.
To hope is to risk despair.
To try is to risk failure.
But the greatest hazard in life is to risk nothing.
The one who risks nothing does nothing—and
finally is nothing.
He may avoid sufferings and sorrow,
But he simply cannot learn, feel, change, grow
or love.
Chained by his certitude, he is a slave: he has
forfeited freedom.
Only one who risks is free.

(Author unknown)

Publishing a book is a risk for me, I wonder if anyone will read it. Joe's surgery was a risk that meant living or dying. There was no other option.

Times between surgeries were definitely precious. One precious day we were enjoying time together. Joey was bouncing on my knee and giving out cuddles. Joey's family watched amusingly as Joey made a game of falling back and forth onto my chest. Joey just loved to play. I began to talk to Joey about the next big surgery. As I spoke lovingly to my Joey I sensed the Lord, His Holy Spirit in an awesome closeness. I felt comforted, as I was unsure who would have the most pain, me or Joe. I reassured my family that the Lord would be with us for the "big one" because the Lord is even here now during our fun time. Peace and happiness were in those precious moments.

Proverb 16:20 (AMP) says, "He who deals wisely and heeds God's word and counsel shall find good, and whoever LEANS on and TRUSTS in and is confident in the Lord—happy, blessed and fortunate is he."

I continued to trust.

Despite my hopes, my heart did break again. I never knew how deep sorrow could be. I never knew how deep love could be all because of one little snowflake. What a *difference* Joey made in my life.

The week prior to heart surgery had its ups and downs. Many thoughts and questions loomed like shadows on the wall. There was tugging in my heart and restlessness. I would think thoughts like, What if this is our last trip together and what if I don't bring Joey home? I had to have a talk with myself, like, "Remember, trust God."

I had to explain to my children that Mommy had to leave again and go to the hospital for their baby brother's operation. It was sad because Joey's sister couldn't understand why she couldn't come along. I explained to her that you have to be sick to go to the hospital and Joey needed his heart fixed, only to have her reply with, "Oh my heart is broken too." I guess she thought if her heart needed fixing she could come along. All of us were hurting in some way.

We do our best but know full-well that troubles come. James 1:2–4 (New International Version) tells us troubles will come: "Consider it wholly joyful, my brethren, whenever you are enveloped in or encounter trails of any sort or fall into various temptations. Be assured and understand that the trail and proving of your faith bring out endurance and steadfastness and patience." It's often God working on us so He can work through us.

All too soon we had our flight to the Vancouver Children's Hospital. The new day brought a new problem. We were up early to a surprise, dense fog. I thought to myself, "The big one (heart surgery) was to be over before Christmas." It dawned upon us that we were at the mercy of the weather. Would we be able to fly out?

I "told" the Lord that it would be good to hurry and lift that fog so we could get on the plane and be on time for our surgery booking. I ended up with an apology prayer, saying, "Lord I'm sorry I was telling you what to do. You reign over the situation, if it's your will for us to go then lift the fog, if it is not then your will still is done."

John 5:14 talks about asking anything in His name according to His will and how He listens and hears. I know that, after the prayer I witnessed the fog start to lift just enough to drive to the airport and by time we reached the airport it was clear, sunny and feeling like a spring day was upon us in November. We had plenty of time to check in our baggage and give Joey's family what would be their last visit. Airports are like hospitals, a place of last visits.

Joey laughed and played with his toy and airplane tickets as we listened for our flight number to be called out, but we couldn't help but overhear another conversation: "I can't believe how the fog cleared up so quickly." I had to chuckle and think,(you get what you pray for). Praying is my norm. I would pray about the fog, the flight safety, the surgery, and everything continually; all the while giving thanks to God who gives life and breath. I didn't always know what was right or wrong to pray for, but God knew my motive.

Thoughts and plane rides are a barricade of constant interruptions. One interruption had to be this rather pleasant lady sitting beside me on the plane. She talked about how her husband had cancer. I started to think about funerals and how tragic to have to prepare one for a lost loved one, someone really close like Joey. Peace attended that interruption as I silently prayed for the stranger.

Doctors said there was an 85 percent chance success rate for heart surgery. I continued to pray for my little snowflake. Life and circumstances are not always about what we want. I know God was close to us at that airport and the hope of success for Joey's heart surgery stayed with me till Joey's very last breath. I never gave up hope.

I was forever learning that God can take all that is good in our lives and weave it together to create a masterpiece. Even when we make bad choices and think we have lost all, God can bring restoration as we pray and wait upon Him. What an adventure to grow in all that God has for us!

I was dreading the "big one," the one the doctors kept calling "high propriety."

Only three months had passed since the last surgery but I tried to be positive, thinking at least the surgery wasn't scheduled at Christmas. I believed the timing was perfect. I believed God had brought him through so much already, how could it be anything but a successful surgery? Instead, I had funeral plans prior to Christmas.

I would have prayed differently and postponed surgery until after Christmas or even canceled it. Two more precious months and one more Christmas would have been heaven to me, but no one could know how much pain Joey was actually experiencing. I certainly couldn't see the whole picture.

The day I was preparing for Joey's final trip to the hospital was peaceful and quiet, but Joey wanted to be held by someone for the whole day, right up to the time of surgery. Darren was carrying Joe about the house and entertaining him as he went. I recall later, after Joe's passing, that I wished I would have carried Joey around a hundred times more but Jesus was preparing a home in heaven for Joe. I believe that Joey's inner spirit told him it was *time* to go home to heaven soon.

I made the most of the time prior to surgery and decided to teach Joey to say "Momma."

Joey gave me his full attention. Joe's eyes watched my lips and in no time at all he said, "Momma." I was so proud and excited. Like a kid with a new toy he repeated Momma" a lot, as if to say, "I got it." This is still a treasured memory.

Chapter 9
Beginning or End?

JOEY WOULD NOT SURVIVE HEART surgery and come home. The last big one was bigger than I guessed. The three months between surgeries was super special; we were finally a normal family doing normal things.

The Bible states in Palms 90:12, "So teach us to number our day that we get us a heart of wisdom." I think I know now what that scripture means,(life is short., so make it count.) The last memory ended in a hospital. I recall my sadness and the eyesore when I stood by Joey's bed. They said the operation went very well but it looked alarming to me.

The lungs seemed fine at first but it was discovered they were badly damaged. That didn't worry me because Joey had survived surgery, the big one, and Joe was a fighter. They explained that the first forty-eight hours was the critical time, mentioning that they had a rough time whereby they had to massage Joey's heart. I think I stopped listening. They said Joey was stable but not in the clear.

Despite all that the doctors told me, the seriousness of it all didn't hit home till I stood beside Joey's hospital bed. Instead of shedding tears I assured his nurse that it would all be fine. I reassured myself, thinking, Joey has an 85 percent chance of survival as per the doctor's prognosis, there's no problem."

I was shocked when I first saw Joey return from the operating room. There were enough wires to make a computer look small time (before laptops). How could such a small body actually withstand all those intravenous lines going into it? And then the seriousness actually became real. To me, my baby looked like a pin cushion.

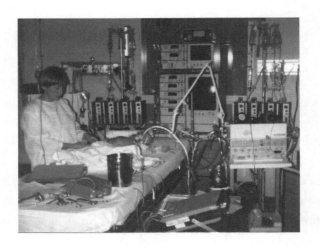

I was alarmed, praying for Joey to pull through.

I quietly held onto Joey's hand, noticing he was starting to awakened. Joey opened his eyes a few times. My heart was breaking as I attempted to pray to my Father God, who I knew never forsakes me and never leaves me. I heard my heart say, "This is my baby, helpless, and I want to love him better."

I remembered that the previous Sunday I had sensed the Lord's presence and requested prayers for Joe's heart surgery. I thought to myself, "God knew both me and Joey would need prayers today."

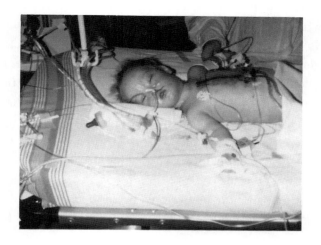

The love of God is such a great love. I remember God's closeness as I remember the very last days with Joey. The nurse said it would not be good if Joey shook off the effect of the sedation too soon, as he needed to rest. Joey lost a lot of blood during his operation and they were quite concerned. Also, Joey was recovering slower than expected.

I thought about all the remarkable recoveries from previous surgeries and tried to reassure myself but I never had all the answers.

As Proverbs 19:21 (AMP) states, "Many plans are in a man's mind but it is the Lord's purpose for him that will stand." Still I cried out in my spirit, "What's Gods plan for Joey? How can pain and suffering happen to children?" At Joey's bedside I just wanted it to be all over.

All I know for sure is that Joey made a *difference* in my life.

I wondered how it must have been for God when his only Son died and suffered. God's plan was for good that the whole world might be saved. I know God loves his Son Jesus as I love my son Joey.

Recovery seemed to worsen with each passing day. There was once when Joey's heart paced on its own otherwise he needed the pacer for backup. Only the grace of God and the power of prayer can help you withstand seeing a precious child suffer. I prayed harder, "God heal my heart, heal Joe's heart and love us through this pain. I know you care. Jesus let me pick up my baby, hold and take away his pain and bring comfort to him."

I knew God heard my prayers and I trusted Jesus was holding Joey as the love of God, the presence of his Holy Spirit moved into that place and time. Joey's big operation was necessary but it would be the last time his little body would be cut open.

I read an article about suffering years ago and it went as follows:

> John 9: "Neither this man nor his parents sinned that he was born blind."
>
> People have believed that a person suffers illness or misfortune because they have sinned. It is a belief connected with the idea that God punishes us when we go against Him. I work as a chaplain and hear troubled people wondering what they have done to deserve illness.
>
> Jesus encountered the same kind of reasoning in His own time. A man who was born blind was assumed to be paying for some sin he had committed, or perhaps even his parents. Jesus said that this blindness was not the result of any sin by anyone.
>
> (Author unknown)

Obviously what we are born with is not due to sin.

The important thing to remember is that God knows our pain and is always with us. God is an ever-present help and was with me and Joe!

At night I returned to my lodging to pray, "God let Joey live." I rested in the idea that God would heal Joey for a witness of a powerful God. I believe that God is always speaking, as he lives in the hearts of those who have accepted Jesus. I was always learning to listen.

I know God speaks through individuals and often children. Joey's brother Darren would on occasion say, "Mom, what would you do if Joey died?" After I thought about it I honestly replied, "Mom would be very sad and cry for a long time, as she would really, really miss Joey." Darren, having a sensitive spirit, answered me with, "I think I would do the same, Mom." There was always a peaceful easy feeling at such moments, almost as if our souls knew the future.

Friends would often make comments that jolted my senses, causing me to wonder, "How long will Joe be here with me?" Yet God's presence was more real than their words.

Joey spent a week in the hospital, for his last time. The last day at the intensive care room I was not myself. I was very shaken up. Usually I could reason away my fears but not this time so I decided on a coffee break. When I returned the clock said 9 p.m. I had left the room for three hours. When I returned I found that Joe's feet were swollen, his toes were a bluish color, and his skin was slightly yellowish. I felt more alarmed than when I left for a break. I left the hospital walking into the night down the street totally perplexed. I had only a few blocks to go to arrive at my lodging, I went directly bed but my mind would not quiet. I began my prayers by giving God orders, praying, "God hurry and make Joey better and let him live and stay with me." Then I thought *stop begging* and thinking out loud I said, "Dear God, I don't know what's happening but You do. Doctors do not give me a straight answer. I cannot understand why it is taking so long for Joey to get better. There have been so many prayers for him yet it is obvious he is not improving. Lord Jesus, I love him so much and I want him to live but your will will be done. And if by chance it is your will to take him home now, please Lord, and make it soon so Joey no longer suffers or has any more pain. Jesus, you know how it hurts to see Joey lying in that hospital in such pain. And please Lord if Joey is going to die, please don't take him home when I am not there, so I can see him one more time." I actually fell asleep in a deep peace.

My thoughts reminded me of an uncomfortable visit from the hospital chaplain. When I listed Joey's condition the minister commented, "Is anything right about him?" I was taken back, as Joey had a whole lot right about him. Joey's physical condition was only stumbling blocks to his health. In reality I thought the chaplain was blind, as Joe overflowed with "unconditional love." God's very presence attended my time with Joseph. Despite his condition he was special, "my *snowflake*."

As the song goes, "He isn't heavy, he's my brother." In this case my God-given child, my baby, was not a burden. Words in songs became alive, as they were often in sync with Bible.

Down syndrome is a condition but this particular chaplain seemed to forget that Joe was first a child of God. Each one of us is special no matter our status; we are all God's creation and He loves us all equally but differently, as we are all snowflakes. God shows no favoritism. And God created Joey.

Joseph was a miracle, a little person filled up with gifts from God his creator. Not a child with a problem but a giver of overflowing love. People often spend their whole lives looking for love until they know God. My Joe was born to love. In the valleys and mountains I went through with Joe it was all about *love*. Awesome love!

I don't think that minister knew he was coming up against a mother bear. I had a calling as a momma. As it turned out God set that chaplain straight, when the minister came by for a second visit Joey convinced him. With a teary eye, the Chaplin commented, "You must really love that little guy." I believe the love in Joey's eyes told the true story. Joey was about his mission, loving people, and he loved the chaplain. "To love the Lord with all our heart and to love our neighbor as ourselves" is the greatest commandment and Joe did it supernaturally everywhere he went.

That last day when the doctor said, "Call your relatives, as it doesn't look good and Joey's heart rate is dropping quickly," I didn't know what to think. The nurse said, "Joey doesn't seem to be responding." And I responded with, "Yes but there's always hope." She said, "I guess so." Even at death's door I hoped and believed there would be a miracle. I stopped and listened, looked and watched the monitors. I sat quietly and sadly and said to myself, "Now you really need hope, faith, and a miracle."

I thought I better phone Joey's family. I remembered I asked the Lord not to let Joey suffer any longer. Basically to heal Joey or take him home. As I started to leave Joey's room I felt a nudging halfway out to go back, which I did instantly. I went back to my baby's bedside, kissed his cheek not once but three times and said goodbye for what was to be the last time. I said, "I'll be back soon!"

As I went to make the phone call I was overwhelmed, I just got to the phone when the doctor behind me said, "Your child is dying." Not really absorbing what he was saying, I looked behind him to where Joey's nurse happened to be and I heard her say, "He died." I thought, "He died?" I really couldn't quite take it in. In shock, I thought, I have to make calls after all.

Before any relatives arrived at the hospital the nurse came and asked if I would like to see Joey. They had removed all the apparatuses and wires when I was phoning. They respectfully gave me a small private room whereby I could be alone with Joey. I could hold him one last time. How could I possibly wrap my mind around what was happening? Here I was holding Joey but this time I had the pain, not my baby. I had held and rocked him so many times but now that was over. The child I loved and cared for became a wound in the deep part of my heart. Now I was the one in need of healing. My tears rolled like a broken dam as I held Joey's little a body that now felt so heavy. I kept checking to see if he was really gone. I wondered how this could be, I must be dreaming, my heart ached for what felt like forever in that moment. I wanted to go back just five minutes so I could tell Joey again how much I loved him. Then I thought, maybe I'll pray and have a miracle and raise the dead. I wasn't as ready as I thought when I prayed for God to take him home instead of seeing him suffer. Time seemed to stand still in that waiting room. Suddenly my thoughts and feelings were interrupted when I noticed blood coming from Joe's eyes and nose. I thought he was hurt because I'd never seen anyone that soon after dying. I was truly confused. How could I possibly give Joe up? Now the questions really began: Where was God? What happened and why? For a moment, I felt very alone.

Thank God for His holy comforter, whose grace is sufficient.

Then I had to learn the true meaning of the words burial, funeral, grief, and dying. I was familiar with death and the loss of loved ones, and I knew a big loving God but this was my son. I loved him with all my heart.

Joey was free from pain and I would always love him and miss him. Joey made a difference in my life. I had God's assurance and peace with His divine presence. Even on this sad day God never left or forsake me. God's comforter was not late. The comforter is always on time.

Christians obviously are not exempt from the trials of this world. Life is a journey of life lessons and my snowflake was a forever-teacher for me. I had God's strength to lean on as I continued to trust. God's word is alive and gives inner strength and I learned again to "trust in the Lord with all your heart and lean not unto your own understanding" (Proverbs 3:5). Life has mountains to climb and it's not always easy. I cannot help but think of this poem:

"What God Hath Promised"

God hath not promised
Skies always blue
Flower strewn pathways
All our life through
God hath not promised
Sun without rain
Joy without sorrow
Peace without pain
But GOD HATH PROMISED
Strength for the day
Rest for the labor
Light for the way
Grace for trials
Help from above
Unfailing sympathy
Undying love.

(Author; Annie Johnson Flint)

Whatever the mountain in life, God keeps His promises. One promise (Isaiah 26:3): "I will keep you in perfect peace who's mine is stayed on thee."

This loss was a mountain to climb but God keeps His word and Gods peace attended my pain. The pain of seeing my babies little body that had just been cut open with a knife was too much to bear alone. I hurt for Joe. When I held Joeys life-less body in my arms the stitches all down his chest were painful to look at. Words cannot describe the helplessness of that moment. My hands were tied and I knew I couldn't fix this one for sure. There were no Band-Aids big enough. God," I cried."This was for sure a mountain. I needed the divine comforter. Only God knew my pain and remained faithful, as His word says, I will not leave you comfortless; I will come to you, (John 14; 18).

One short week after his surgery, Joey's suffering ended and mine began. Joey went home to be with Jesus and I missed him! Joey had his healing when he left that hospital bed and all his pain was gone.

I was sad for a long time. I got through because of the grace of God and His almighty goodness. What a major *difference* Joey made in my life, a *perfect* little *snowflake*!

Joey's real home in heaven was calling his name. Joey did teach lessons on unconditional love when he lived in our home. Joey's birth brought a special understanding of unconditional love and his death left me dreaming about his happiness in his real home in heaven, as per John 14:2 (AMP): "In my Father's house are many dwelling places (homes). If it were not so, I would of told; for I am going to prepare a place for." To know he was happy would make everything okay. As a family we all enjoyed getting to know Joey's loveable personality. Joey had a spirit that made us all watch in awe, as he put up with so much pain and struggled with learning new things. Joey's Heavenly Father was ever-present. Joey's unconditional love and the gift of love that Joey left me was maybe his soul mission.

There was a void when our angel went to heaven but we moved forward as Christian soldiers. 11 Timothy 3 says, "You must endure hardship as a good soldier of Christ" and verse 11 "for if we died with Him, we shall also live with Him" and verse 12 "If we endure we shall also reign with Him."

I cried a lot, reliving last talks with Joe. After his heart surgery I whispered in his ear,

"Joey, we're all waiting for you to get better because Christmas is almost here and Momma has a secret. I got you a Koala bear that you are just going to love." My mind interrupted as I realized Joey was going home in an ambulance and I'd take the plane. Joey wouldn't see his Christmas gifts waiting for him. Reality was Joey had a flight to heaven and I needed an ambulance for my heartache.

I missed my precious snowflake!

"Heaven Is for Real" is a movie about a child's visitation to heaven and it confirmed to me how happy Joe must be in his heavenly home. I secretly hoped he missed me.

Grieving was all a part of Joe passing. His brother Darren said he was scared that he would leave us or we would leave him. I reassured Darren we would see Joey again one day in heaven. We all needed time and God's comforter to carry through the grief of losing Joe.

God was not silent during our grief, He sent His comforter.

One of my favorite pastimes is enjoying Christmas lights. One night after Joe passed I had a dream that he was home for Christmas and sharing a Christmas light extravaganza with me. After watching, a move, "Heaven is for Real" I am positive the heavenly lights outshine any here on earth. "The entirety of heaven is lit up and there is no darkness" (Ezek. 32:8).

Going home to heaven will be the trip of all trips. How very awesome to be with Jesus and to know that all children go to be with Him. My mother (about three months prior to her death) said she heard an audible voice that spoke the words, "Going home to be with Jesus." The Lord announced her homecoming invitation to her personally.

I can only imagine all the special announcements when one enters heaven.

Details do not get by God. In my personal experiences I can see how God is in the business of preparing. God did prepare me in my heart of hearts. I can only imagine how Jesus prepared His own earthly family for His death and resurrection. Jesus prophesied it to all His friends, followers, and family.

In the early days of grieving the loss of Joey, I prayed that the Lord would show me that Joey was ok and God did. I had a vision of Joe smiling (with a grin ear to ear), walking and peeking around the corner at me. Joe said, "Hi Mom." Joey was too happy for me to wish him back. I could sense and feel happiness that can only be described as heavenly.

A hospital stay with Joey would be a welcomed time in comparison to the grief of losing a child. Yet I knew the power and strength that lay in the attitude of thankfulness. I was extremely thankful for the precious gift of Joey's siblings. I am thankful forever for God's faithfulness.

Christmas was a mere month away and I would be busy. We all felt the absence of Joey's presence. Darren was only nine and Desiree barely three, and Joey was a big part of their life. One day in December not long after Joey's funeral, Darren blurted out, "We should adopt a baby with Down syndrome." We all missed him!

I surrendered Joey to God. That was my final prayer before Joe's passing. Joe left that hospital bed for his heavenly home the very next morning and it was right after one more bedside visit. I know God gave Joe his first breath but not a last breath, as Joe just stepped over into eternal heaven with a new healed body. Joe is very alive in heaven.

Every Christmas is a reminder that Joseph died one month prior to Christmas. I would say Joey received a gift early, the gift of a new heavenly home.

I would sometimes imagine Joey in heaven, imagination gave me comfort. Thinking and trying to put pieces of the puzzle together left me frustrated. I would remind myself a lot that "Joey is in Jesus' hands" and the frustration would pass, questions would diminish, and peace would come.

Matthew 28:2 says, "Cast your cares on the Lord and he will give you rest." This is always the answer and in reality that's what I did. All along I knew that closing my mind to endless questions was the best idea and helped frustration. God had everything in hand.

We had attended a Christmas party the previous Christmas and we were invited back even though Joey had passed. When Joe and I went to the previous year's party we sat beside a mother and her son, Kurtis. Little did we know that before another Christmas rolled around both our sons wouldn't be on our laps, but instead on Jesus' lap celebrating heaven in all its glory. Kurtis seemed to have his share of pain in his life also but freedom and no pain were at his doorstep. Peace and eternal love were to be those two boys' gifts for next Christmas. What awesome joy they have for all eternity. Two little snowflakes who met on earth and heaven!

God has given us all many little snowflakes. Many snowflakes go to heaven early. God is an eternal God so really what is early in light of eternity?

I remember a friend of mine who also had a son with Down syndrome. My friend would have moms meet at her home for support. One particular meeting we were all discussing the special-ness of children and how they were also different with or without Down syndrome. Both my friend and I were moms of three chil-dren. We were sharing from our hearts how each of our children are special gifts. We *all loved* our children the same and didn't see the condition of Down syndrome but the instead the uniqueness of the child.

Don't Clone a Snowflake!

Joseph was my youngest and Heather was the youngest in my friend's family. Kurtis was also at this meeting. Little did we know from our small group that three of the children among us would be in heaven before next Christmas, Heather died from a tragic accident.

Heather's mom supported me after Joey's death in a letter. I feel it may encourage some readers, as people need people. The letter is below:

Dear Becky,

I'm glad I talked with you earlier today. You have been on my mind and in my prayers since I heard of Joey's death. When Heather died, the love and caring of so many people seemed to be an expression of God's love for us at that time. I have never felt the power of prayer as strongly as at that time. One letter we received particularly helped to sustain us and I'd like to share part of it with you. No words, no explanations, no fancy theories help now. I believe God's love for Joey has not changed nor His purpose for him. I see Joey going on from strength to strength even though the way in which his life will develop will have to be different because he will no longer have the particular body that your love gave him for his existence on this earth.

Remember that all the beauty, all the joy, all the laughter that was Joey still is. He is still a radiant, living, loving, person. Only his body and the existence we know on this level are changed. He is more alive than ever, his eyes seeing more than we can see, his heart loving more than we can love. We can only let him go, that God may lift him, love him, fulfill his high goals in and for him.

The man who wrote these words for us was our minister when Dennis was a newborn. He helped us a great deal at that time. I am enclosing a poem that helped me get through days and months after Heather's death. The enclosed money is for you to purchase your "big picture" of Joey, a memory to cherish.

May God's strength and comfort heal and lift you
and grant you peace; sincerely, your friend.

P.S. Peace can take a long time coming. Please give
me a call anytime you feel like a visit.

I was encouraged. We had an understanding that only moms
who have lost a child come to truly know.

With Jesus precious little snowflakes are well taken care of.

When I was standing at Joseph's grave I couldn't help but notice
all the babies' graves.

Beside Joseph's grave was a gravestone named Joseph, the same
age. I never had money for a marker but it was marked in my mind.
I reminded myself "Jesus thinks of everything."

Tragic as it is to lose a child, the truth that they are without
pain, happy, walking and playing in God's kingdom brings comfort.

The very last day Joey had on earth had relief in one way: no
more hospitals. Freedom for Joe! The doctors did all that was possible to save Joey's life and I am grateful. I wanted Joe here yet
I am happy knowing he is now happy. Trusting God for a positive outcome is not easy when someone's life is on the line. Yet
faith grows even stronger in the worst of challenges. Even the day
Joe left for heaven I was blessed. The Lord answered my prayer to
visit Joe one last time and I knew Joe had a big party waiting for
him above.

The doctors said Joey would have lost his fingers and toes
had he survived the heart surgery; surely a small price to live, but
another challenge to overcome. I honestly thought, "No big deal,
as I serve a God of miracles and God would have grown new ones."
I felt sorrier for the doctors than Joe as I thought, "Wait till they
meet the great physician Jesus." I knew blessings and a new beginning was around the corner. That's what Joe got, a new beginning

with all new fingers and toes and the supernatural blessing of a new body.

Revelation 20:4 says, "God will wipe away every tear from their eyes; and Death shall be no more; neither shall there be anguish (sorrow and mourning) nor grief nor pain anymore, for the old conditions and the former order of things have passed away. Yes eye has not seen or hear has not heard the great and awesome things God has planned for His children." Our pain here on earth is nothing in comparison to all eternity. *Life is but a vapor and Eternity is forever.* So really, is death a beginning or an end? I love Joe and will always miss him and would have laid down my life for him. God's love tells me I'll meet Joe again sooner than I think.

In the meantime, I have my own personal "remembrance days." I can pull memories out of my heart at will after years have passed. All the while I remain thankful that Jesus loved me enough to die for me and that I have hope of an eternal home.

One day soon after Joey's passing I sensed closeness to Joe. I knew Joe was just over on the other side of the door waiting for us to join him. This, I believe, was a beginning of my healing. My mourning began to be turned into praise as per the Bible; Isaiah 61:3 says, "God will console those who mourn in Zion, give beauty for ashes and the oil of joy for mourning." God's promises began to be my healing. Healing is a promise for us, as that's why Jesus died on the cross. By His stripes we are healed.

Because of God's love I've grown in many ways. I've learned how weak our mortal flesh can be. But thankfully my vision of others is becoming what God would have it be. This is to love the seemingly unlovable and those who are needy. I thank God that I can walk with Him and experience a "greater vision" outside of my little world.

When one is born again into God's world, we as weak vessels (people) can say we are strong, in reality that's what happens in and through the power of God's Holy Spirit living within us as believers.

Believers have a hope in a real living Savior, the hope of the world to give eternal life.

Acts 2:21 (AMP) says, "And everyone who calls upon the name of the Lord shall be saved." Acts 4:12 says, "Neither is there salvation in any other; for there is no other name under heaven given among men, by which we must be saved."

I can smile in my spirit when I think of all of *God's snowflakes in Heaven.* What a glorious reunion to meet treasured family and friends in heaven. I hope to bring many lost ones with me to heaven as I share Jesus in Joe's story. Children already have their ticket to heaven and God didn't clone any of them. My great niece, Shakira, at the age of eight years used her ticket to heaven early due to a tragic accident. I am looking forward to our meeting in heaven. The mother, (as it is with many), left behind had her life changed with the loss of her daughter. I know for certain minor issues are no longer important to her. Family and loved ones become dearer to all who lose a close loved one.

As a grandma now I have to brag some. One Sunday my grandson Aden, who was just seven years old at the time, was asked to pray at the beginning of a Sunday school class. Aden prayed for families, for the lost, and to have fun. I believe he covered all of the basics. Talk about wisdom out of the mouth of babes. When families get it right and live for God they will influence the whole world and enjoy life during the journey.

Aden 10 years old with grandma.

My favorite times of enjoyment in life are simple things like laughing with children. My Joey had the most contagious laugh that totally tickled my heart. Joe's sister, Desiree, would tickle Joe's tummy to make him giggle. Simple things are the very best times in life, not necessarily seeing all the sights of the world like the Grand Canyon but instead enjoying the gift of a new day.

I love memories with my young children. One time while watching my children play, Joey happened to be sitting in his high chair and had his hands folded as if in prayer. I used that little thing to teach my children to pray, or maybe Joey was just about His heavenly fathers business, again!

God wants us to enjoy our children as we work and learn with them. I loved even little bath times with Joey, as he was so happy. Everyday moments can be sacred when enjoyed with God as our friend. As I put in time my relationship becomes closer to God.

I was surely blessed and wished I could overhear what Joey is talking to Jesus about. Is he calling me his momma?

After Joe's passing, I began the process of sorting through items of Joe's. There were both good and bad days. Finding papers such as Joey's physiotherapy exercises, his baby blessing, and poems always brought back a flood of memories. The therapy exercises were to help give Joe a head start. I quote "a better quality of life." That was for Joe's physical growth. Joe's spiritual inner self was already perfection and that's what counts with God.

An attitude of thankfulness was a stronghold to carry me during the grieving of Joe.

I was thankful Joey had a baby blessing. A baby blessing, for those who don't know, is a prayer of dedication to the Lord. The part that spoke the loudest to me is the words "Joseph will play a major role in your spiritual life." Joey was blessed on his birthday in the hospital incubator as doctors were unsure if Joey was going to survive. On that very first day of his life, words spoken over Joey during his blessing were "Joey is already ministering to that round about him. And the Lord has His hand on Joseph's life." Joey wasted no time in saying, "I am here now and I am going to make every day count." Awesome it was and awesome in retrospect.

In my collection of Joey's items I found a poem I wrote to myself. I wrote about how I no longer loved the season of autumn, but preferred winter. I know that when I wrote it I was grieving my loss because autumn was full of memories. Putting my thoughts on paper was therapy.

The poem expressed what was in my heart; simple but true. I still prefer winter because of the memories attached to a sadder time in autumn.

Seasons did change in my life but I'm glad that God does not change.

Philippians 4:7 (New International Version) says, "Be anxious for nothing, but in everything by prayer and supplication, with all thanksgiving, let your requests be made known to God and the peace of God, which surpasses all understanding will guard your hearts and minds through Jesus Christ."

God did just that, as in His word He guarded my heart that went into the casket, He guarded my thoughts with His peace. I only had a moment in time when I looked out the window on that autumn day and wrote down my thoughts. But as always, the peace of God ruled in my heart of hearts. Memory lane had its share of heartaches yet peace reigned. In the beginning days of Joe's passing I would wake up in the morning thinking he was in his crib and when I would hear a plane flying over I'd relive my last plane ride with Joey. It was a new beginning of sorts to learn to live without my baby boy. I would deliberately choose to think about Joey's trip to heaven. It had to be first class with a high-ranking angel when he lifted off to his eternal home, because Joe was a snowflake and there was only one of him in the world.

Life carried on. Robert Frost said, "One thing I know for sure, Life goes on."

Joe's sister filled my day and we loved playing "pat a cake." I accidentally sang J for Joey instead of G for God and little Desiree noticed, responding with "poor Joey, he died" and "why don't you go get him?" How I wished. She was used to Joey being gone and assumed mommy could just go again to pick him up. I said, "Desi, we have to wait till it's our turn to go to heaven." Desiree understood what taking turns meant and seemed satisfied with explanation. We ended having another peaceful silence, a little incident was another sacred moment. God's love was ever-present in my struggling to completely accept Joe's death.

One day when we went to a professional, genetic doctor I especially recall the powerful love of God. I could hardly listen to the factual statistics he was listing off. Yet I sensed something else. The doctor's prognosis meant nothing to me. But it began to tear up my heart and I could hardly hold back the tears. And then and there the Holy Spirit reigned and had the last say with peaceful words that said, Joe's is in God's hands and you have no need to be anxious. God was in control, reigning in my heart. I was in awe of the last say from my God. The doctor's negative attitude about Down syndrome children was overpowered by the overpowering love and presence of the Holy Spirit. I wish I had said loud and clear:

Don't clone a snowflake.

Having Down syndrome doesn't mean all are the same.

In reality only God knew it all.

God gave me strength in the beginning and closures.

Joe was the gift that made a *difference* in my life and my walk with God. Joe was a special gift, not at all a child with a special problem. Down syndrome individuals may have similar physical traits but are still different like snowflakes in their personalities just like everyone else. God has purpose and plan for every single person He created. Acceptance is the key to give unconditional love. I learned to love for those I pray for. We have no excuse not to love one another, with or without a disability. Praying is knocking on the door of love. Growing is a process to become more like Christ.

God is eternal and every day is a new beginning. My desire is to love others as Christ loves me. I believe if my heart gets full of many to love, God will just make more room in my heart because Jesus lives in me.

Forgetting the past, all things become new, as Colossians 3:10 says, "And clothe yourselves with the new (spiritual self) which is (ever in the process of being) renewed and remolded into (fuller and more perfect knowledge upon) knowledge after (the likeness of Him who created it.)"

Psalm 37:23 says, "The steps of a righteous man are directed and established by the Lord when he delights in His way (and he busies himself with his every step.) Though he falls he will not be utterly cast down, for the Lord grasps his hand in support and holds him up."

I shall continue to grow in His awesome eternal love. Daily I put off my old self and focus on God's word. My self-image is no longer an issue, but what is important is how God sees me and all handicapped individuals. I discovered my specialness, just as I know my Joey is.

There is no end with Jesus and his clock ticks different from mine. August 14 would have been Joe's thirty-fifth birthday and I had to go to the hospital for an infection. I had a four-hour wait, which can give loads of time to think. I was here in this same hospital thirty-five years ago giving birth to Joey on the same date. Earlier that day in a restroom the song "In the Garden" was playing. I knew God was whispering, "I am with you and I know you remember Joey today." The doctor in emergency got to hear Joe's story, thirty-five years later. That was yesterday and so was Joe's life here on earth, but now a new day brings new beginnings.

Awe to have met and loved a *snowflake*!

Chapter 10
A Funeral

WHEN THE DAY CAME TO plan my son's funeral I'd thought, "Can I cancel?" Unfortunately funerals don't come with that option. Joey's father was ill so God sent me my own special handmaiden (my sister) to assist with the funeral plans. We went to the funeral home to check it out and I decided to have Joe's casket in a separate room during the funeral service. I thought that way I might be able to listen to the speaker instead of staring at Joe's casket. My request was denied, as the director said there would be no other room available. I was discouraged but at the same time decided the Lord would be my support and it would work out. It turned out the plane with Joe's body couldn't land in time for the service, so the casket wasn't even in the building for the funeral ceremony, just as I had wished. Joe's body arrived later. I was thankful to be able to focus on my children instead of a casket. My son, Darren, sat next to me shedding the most tears. My children needed me as much as I needed them. We all grieved Joey.

In the morning of the funeral day, we went to the florist shop. I picked out yellow roses with daises and baby breath flowers to compliment the bouquet. It was perfect!

I was aware of God taking me through this funeral preparation and all the little details.

All people are different like flowers and snowflakes, but put together make something beautiful. My florist was just as helpful as Joey's nurses were. Maybe another of God's special handmaidens!

I took pictures of Joe's casket bouquet and later dried some flowers to save for a keepsake. We hung onto a few of Joey's special items for memory sakes: a snoopy bank, pictures, and a Bible. The gift of love was the legacy Joey left us.

Joe's legacy was God's expression of love. I was privileged to have Joseph live long enough to lend an experience of a pure love relationship. Love is a give and receive process, thus a relationship.

My neighbor was gifted with a listening ear. She received a few "sermons about Joey, love and Jesus."

It was all about Jesus.

A little snowflake brought blessings and miracles and a funeral, but mostly *love*.

Don't Clone a Snowflake!

2 Corinthians 12:29 goes as follows: "Three times I pleaded with the Lord to take it away from me." (I pleaded many times for Joe's healing.) "But He said, 'My grace is sufficient for you, for my power is made perfect in weakness.' Therefore I will boast more gladly about my weakness, so that Christ's power may rest on me." That is why for Christ's sake I delight in weakness, in insults, in hardships, in persecutions, in difficulties, for when I am weak I am strong.

With God's grace I had the strength to survive Joe's funeral. I became a strong survivor in my struggles and in turn was able to help others. Sorrows never have to be wasted. I do not believe for a minute that it is a blessing for one's child to die but I believe blessings can come from it. There is a big difference, (with Jesus); we are blessed to enter into a greater relationship with the Holy Spirit, a comforter, and to know for sure that a loved one is in paradise. And know without a doubt that we will see our loved one again all because of Jesus.

The loss is heartache but temporary, paradise is forever. I cannot put into words the heartaches of losing Joey. Many times I wished for Joey back just to see him smile one more time. I took comfort in knowing Joey had no more pain. The pain of losing a loved one is very real. Many asked why a good God would let a child die and why he doesn't just heal them all.

I believe we should never give up on God, as he won't give up on us. Many have been miraculously healed after a very long time. Also, remember when a child needs healing and dies, they are healed in heaven forever.

Funerals really are not an end but a new beginning for those who passed and those left behind.

God is all-knowing and to even imagine His greatness would be more than one could imagine. I heard a story once about how awesome and powerful God is. The story said try to imagine if you were all-powerful God and everyone was ants and God wanted to communicate with the ants. God first would have to become one because the ability to understand wouldn't happen. So that's why God became a man, to communicate with us His creation. I know we are created in God's image and we are not ants but it helped me to know how vast God's greatness is.

How Great Thou Art!

I leaned into the knowing that my Joey was now in eternity and it helped heal the pain and deep wound. Jesus' wounds on the cross were unimaginably painful yet had an eternal purpose. And God the Father healed Jesus' wounds. It is too much to understand in our mortal state.

How does one even fathom the vast universe? I heard lately that scientists have finally concluded there's a God. If they had just asked God he would have saved them the trouble of research.

For me knowing Joe is with God in paradise gave me strength to do a funeral, to grieve and go on in life. But it took time.

I love the following poem.

"Friend of a Wounded Heart"

Smile makes them think you are happy.
Lie and say things are fine and hide that
empty longing,
That you feel, don't ever show it.
Just keep your heart concealed.
Why are the days so lonely?
I wonder where, where can the heart go free,
And who will dry the tears that no one sees
There must be someone to share your dreams.

Caught like a leaf in the wind, looking for
a friendship.
Where could you turn?
Whisper; speak the words of a prayer
And you will find Him there, arms open wide,
Love in His eyes!
Jesus, He meets you where you are,
Jesus, He heals your secret scars.
All the love you're longing for is
Jesus is the friend of a wounded heart.
Joy comes in the morning and hope deepens as
you grow,
And peace beyond the reaches of your soul comes
Flowing through you.
For LOVE has made you whole.

(Writers; Wayne Watson, Claire Cloninger)

I believe everything in heaven is governed by love. May it be done on earth as it is in heaven!

I had regrets. The most prominent one was that I was not beside Joey the very moment of his death. I thought I should have been holding his hand. I think I believed I was entitled to see angels carry Joe off. I suppose I was thinking selfishly, as pain can do that. Blessings overshadowed regrets.

The Bible says in Psalm 107:2 "Give thanks to the Lord for His goodness, and for His wonderful works to the children of men."

God is a good God.

I can truly always remain thankful. Despite not holding Joe's hand for his last parting moment, I am thankful for I know a sweet band of angels carried him home even if I didn't get a peek.

I am thankful for all the smallest joys and my treasures: loved ones, happy memories, and above all, the joy of the Lord.

Grieving seemed to come in waves. I was assured that reunion day would come in a blink and that Joey was absent from me but present with God. That is the reality. My God did turn my mourning into joy, as I know we will run to each when I see Joe again!

Chapter 11
Reality—Life Goes On

HOW LONG DOES ONE GRIEVE? I didn't know but I was happy to see summer arrive, finally a new season. It was now three summers since Joe was born.

Joey's very first summer was half over when he was born and half of his second summer was spent in the hospital for his colostomy reversal. This third year would have finally been a summer Joe would have really enjoyed. I was sad thinking about that but he was now in heaven, down by the "river of life." The first of everything was kind of sad for me, so I would pray to be busy.

As it happened, without looking, I found myself with an at-home babysitting job. A little toddler came into our lives, the same age as my Joey would have been. Warren was happy jolly little guy and we all adored him. Desiree and I (despite her age) would take turns cuddling lovable Warren. I was happier busy.

One particular day Desiree and I had the duty of taking Warren for his inoculation at the health unit which turned out to be an interesting social event. We knew the health nurse as she used to visit Joey.

Children are little beacons of faith and honesty and Warren brought a ray of sunshine into our hearts as we grieved Joey.

After our visit to the health unit our day continued with a stopover at the mall. Little Desiree decided she was going to push Warren's stroller on the walk. I enjoyed watching the "little mothering" in my little girl. Warren happened to be holding a toy in his lap, which fell out of his hands. A sales clerk retrieved it saying, "Here, give it to your little brother." I really didn't know whether to laugh or cry. How could the nice lady have known I was a grieving mother? The scripture Proverbs 14:13 rang true this day: "Even in laughter the heart may sorrow."

Warren was like Desiree's little brother while his mom was at work and Joe, her brother, was in heaven. I had both laughter and sorrow that moment in time.

Mothering didn't end when grieving Joe. Darren had asthma and Desiree had health concerns. One minute moms are tying shoes, another minute we're teaching and hugging. I prayed a lot!

Would grief end? I didn't know!

Routines in life filled my time and there never seemed to be enough time. Yet the Lord took time to encourage me and I could hear His still voice say, "You have many mothering days ahead of you and Joey is fine with me." That was the reality long after I have entered into grandma land.

Sleepless nights did come and I'd awakened to a pillow soaked with tears. I believe as long as I live I will miss my precious "snowflake" but not in a sad way, because of my Savior, friend and healer Jesus.

Putting down my thoughts and feelings on paper was therapy for my grief. I was not thinking at the time that I would make it into this book. It was my little journal and my personal "book of memories." I did not want to forget anything!

I had to let go of guilt over little stuff. I was sorry I spent time immersed in a book on Joey's last two days at home. As a grieving parent, I wished I could have done more for Joey. I know I did the best that I could at the time so guilt had to leave. The most difficult reality I ever faced was the death of my son. Reality is shock, guilt, grief when death comes knocking. Too many of us think we have forever here but that's not reality.

Reality takes on many faces. Our mortality is shaken when natural disasters occur.

Earthquakes are a reality. I was in Hawaii in March 2011 when Japan had the major earthquake. I was already in a deep sleep when I heard voices say, "You must leave now for higher ground." When I awoke, I experienced "shock" and the reality of the uncertainty of life and death. Many died from the magnitude of that earthquake. The Lord warned me in a dream the first night in Hawaii. In my dream I saw deep freezers with rotten meat, heads with bandages, and no water. The reality that life can suddenly end happened in Japan that tragic day. Sadly, there many were left with only grief.

That day I wrote a letter to Jesus.

Dear Father,

I thank you today that my dream came true to see the beautiful island of Maui, Hawaii. Thank you that my greatest trip is yet to happen. When you return and take me to heaven.

Thank you Father for the revelation you gave me in Hawaii that nothing in this world is as important as time well spent. Thank you that I enjoy the little things, like a park. Thank you for the privilege of being a wife, mother and a grandma.

The pearls of jewelry here are beautiful but I know the real pearls of worth are wisdom and contentment with godliness. The world cannot offer me what I found in you. I thank you today Father for bringing me into a closer walk with you. I pray that as your daughter you will use me to further your kingdom here on earth in these last days and that many will come into salvation. Bless and keep my family under the cover of your wings forever.

I love you with all my heart and soul. Rebecca

I meant every word. The Japanese disaster was a reality check for many people and a reminder for me. Life can be cut short!

Reality said, "I could always find something to be thankful about and even though in the first year of Joey's passing I went through a valley I was thankful to God for His faithfulness."

That year I also turned thirty years of age. And I am now completing the book I started thirty years ago. I am sixty-three years young, looking forward to a long life yet in awe of how quickly time flew by.

I pray to continue to love aggressively yet wisely as I continually grow in the awesome eternal love of Jesus.

I am still wondering where thirty years went.

When I looked over my shoulder, the first year after losing and missing Joey was gone. I experienced the "firsts": the first birthday without him, the death anniversary, and the seasons. Taking one day at a time was a determined choice as in reality we can do almost anything for just one day. Joey's first birthday without him was a reality check. I must have mentioned it as little Desiree said, out of the blue in a grownup way, "Mommy where's Joey?" I curiously asked, "You mean our Joey, Mommy's Joey?" (Desiree's friend next door was also named Joey.) She replied, "Yes!" in a loud firm voice. Desiree always had a surprising way of making her voice known. I reminded her that our Joey is now in heaven. Little Desiree responded with "Oh yeah, he's in heaven; we can have his birthday anyway." We had cake!

The Father in heaven helped me to walk through all the firsts and with time I could walk without help.

During my year of "firsts" I decided I should do something for myself and joined an aerobics class. One night at the class a group of five mentally challenged individuals joined us. I really had no interaction with any adults with disabilities prior to this. At the time in my limited experience I thought I was normal and these ones were different, but now through years of working in group home I wonder if there is a definition for normal. We are all snowflakes and different. In my ignorance I did clone those five individuals that night. I was unsure of how to respond so as my norm I said to myself, "Trust God." I now believe God was introducing me to what would become my life's work. The class turned out to be a beautiful evening as I recognized the presence of the Lord as the five newcomers settled into doing our exercises. I was overwhelmed with the love of God for our visitors and I sensed angels around us. I thought again of the Bible verse that says, "Be careful as many of you have entertained angels unawares." I'm still not sure nor do I really care. They seemed childlike and a presence covered them. I know it was the love of Jesus. Jesus so loved these individuals. I know better now, we all are *snowflakes*. It was awesome how one challenged individual decided to end that exercise class with the Lord's Prayer.

Don't Clone a Snowflake.

I never dreamed at that season of my life that I would ever work in a group home. I just knew I loved snowflakes.

Being around the mentally challenged adults reminded me of a conversation I had when Joe was born. The doctor encouraged me to put Joey in an institution. My son has Down syndrome but being separated from his family would never be his problem. I couldn't believe a doctor saying, "Joey would be better off." What baby is better off without a mom? I suppose many parents did listen to doctors, as maybe they felt unqualified to raise a handicapped child. I hope parents have become aware of the support available to them raising their own child. Many parents have been misinformed and should never feel guilty for their choices. Often outside help makes all the difference to care for their disabled child, as reality is that sometimes it can bring extreme stress. I believe as long as the child is not forgotten by families they have a chance to grow and develop. Adoption can be a good choice. Every situation is unique.

The reality of it all is that we don't know the real reality of one's circumstances until we walk in their shoes. If we did we would have a lot more people living the life of being "our brother's keepers." And awakened to the Bible verse Matthew 25:40, "If you do it to the least of these you do it unto me." If everyone came into understanding that little things make a big difference and random acts of kindness actually "shape lives"—it's called the "compound effect"—little acknowledgments and positive attitudes would make a big difference in the value of every life. I believe disabilities are opportunities to learn to love. At an exercise class I saw the innocence and vulnerability of those who society may look down upon, and the purity of their spirit and character.

Who can judge anyone God created? We first should walk a mile in their shoe to keep our perception and attitude in the right place. I never knew that I would get a lesson on love at an exercise class. I remember that after the class a man returned and like a perfect gentlemen, poked his head around the corner and with a catchy big smile said, "Goodnight ladies." Made me think things like: "How much do they know? Does anyone really know? Are they Gods special agents?" It raised my eyebrows. I wished more men acted that way.

During my first year of grieving Joey, I experienced divine appointments. God has His own university. I learned "all things work together for those who love God." I had questions in my grief but I knew God sees "the whole picture." My foundation in Christ "kept me." I could never explain or understand it all and all my inspirations, articles, poems, and dreams could not sustain me.

They were band aids. My foundation of faith in a living God is what remained throughout the grief and all my "whys."

God knew what I needed before I even asked. In my sorrow I could be thankful for all the blessings and lessons in God's university, "Joey's story." I learned that all children are extra special to Jesus. In Matthew 19:14 Jesus says, "Leave the children alone, allow the little ones to come to Me, and do not forbid or restrain or hinder them for of such (as these) is the kingdom of heaven composed." Jesus said this when the disciples tried to keep children back from Him.

The ultimate love story was demonstrated by God the Father, who gave His only begotten Son, that whosoever believeth in Him shall not perish; but have everlasting life. For God sent not His son into the world to condemn the world; but that through him the world might be saved.

God giving his Son to die on the cross so all mankind may be saved was love in action.

In this world in my mortal body I experienced grieving. I would see people whose only connection with them was Joey (divine appointments). During a hospital visit I bumped into Joey's physiotherapist. We hugged and I'm sure we both remembered Joe. Memories returned of the not-too-distant past. Once home I stared at the floor where Joe used to do his physiotherapy and muttered "Joey where are you?" I let the tears come, as I loved my Joey. The reality was I met people who also loved Joey, for surely Joey's love lived on. I would dream Joey was asking for me with "Where is my momma?" I like to believe Joey also misses his family.

Grieving did not last. Putting my hope in God was in reality the answer. Not only is God faithful in times of grieving but in all the disasters that come upon the earth. Like the old hymn states, "The things of the world will become strangely dim in the light of His awesome love."

When I was grieving I wrote down Joey's story. I call it grief therapy.

Soon after Joeys passing I attended church, where the pastor was "laying on his hands" in prayer for a baby. This baby had successfully come through three heart surgeries. I experienced a sincere peacefulness that said to my heart, Yes, Joey did not survive his heart surgery but he's in his heavenly home. After the service the pastor's wife gave to me the following poem:

"Safely Home"

I am home in heaven, dear ones,
Oh so happy and so bright
There is perfect joy and beauty
In this everlasting light.
All the pain and grief is over,
Every restless tossing passed.
I am now at peace forever;
Safely home at last.
Therefore you must not grieve so sorely,
For I love you dearly still.
Try to look beyond earths shadows.
Pray to trust our Fathers will,
There is still work waiting for you,
So you must not idly stand.
Do it now while life remaineth,
You shall rest in Jesus hand.
When that work is all completed
He will gently call you home,
Oh the rapture of that meeting,
Oh the joy to see you come.

(The pastor's wife personalized the poem with:
LOVE for all-eternity JOEY.)

Sometimes I would grieve in dreams. I loved my dreams that
felt like little visits with Joey. I loved talking about my baby. Some
well-meaning family would tell me that I should be thankful for
the two beautiful children I still had. I couldn't understand how
they would think I wasn't. I was more than thankful for my children, family, and friends. My loving children were special also but
the truth remained that no one could replace the loss of Joey. There
would always be one Joseph, one Desiree, one Darren. All special
snowflakes are so different yet so very special. Each of them had a
special spot in my heart.

In John 14:27 it reads, "Peace I leave with you, My peace I give
to you, not as the world gives do I give to you."

The Bible brings life and healing and I could enjoy my living
children because of God's peace, even during grieving.

Joseph's life was likened to a ministry. Joe gave out freely life
lessons on love. A popular saying is "Carry On." My favorite is
"Love God and Carry On."

I kept mementos to help me remember precious times with
Joe. In reality stuff had to be given away. Parting of items did help
with letting go and moving forward. It brings some closure, as does
a funeral.

I'm continually working to become more and more rooted in
God's love. I pray those readers who are now grieving a loss will
receive hope knowing *God* is *good* and no matter what He will
work all things together for our good if we but let Him.

In the storms of life we have an anchor, a lighthouse called Jesus
the Savior of the world. Today with all the problems in the world
one needs an anchor, truth, and a sure foundation. Living in the
love and truth of a good God brings the world hope and direction.
The hope is that it may be done on earth as it is in heaven.

God wants to be involved in all we do, whether it's little stuff or bigger stuff. The little things like giving your baby a bath or the bigger stuff when a doctor says, "Your baby with Down syndrome may never talk" and then he says, "Momma." Jesus dumfounds the experts. Now that is big stuff to a mom of a special needs baby.

One day not too long after Joey's passing, a friend was praying for me when she had a vision. In the vision she saw Joey sitting on Jesus' lap and Joey told Jesus that he missed his momma. Only I and Joey and Jesus knew at this time we had been working on that momma word.

I lived in the moment when packing away Joe's personal items, taking time to read poems I saved. This one was from Joe's funeral service:

"In Memory"

What do you mean by this weeping to break my
very heart?
We are both in Christ's keeping and therefore
cannot part.
You there, I here, though parted, we still at heart
are one.
I'm only just in sunshine, the shadow scarcely gone.
What can the brightness see, is only a little way that
leads you to me. I was so very weary,
Sure you would not mourn, that I a little sooner
should lay my burden down.
So weep not my darling, God wipes away all tears.
It's only a little way, though you may call it years.

Well it has been forty years now so it must be a lot closer to when I can see my Joe again. I enjoyed divine appointments with both strangers and friends during my grief. It was refreshing during the sad time of letting go of Joe's belongings. Joe's infant development worker called during one of these times. She talked about Joey and how she was always so impressed with Joey, saying, "Joey always seemed to want to communicate so much with his vocalizations and smiles." Her praise was music to my ears and she loved Joey too!

Joey was a snowflake and his middle name to me was "*Love*." The early days of grief were busy and I had much peace due to the awesome difference he made in my life. I met new people; I learned new things and felt the love of so many.

One of the special items of Joe's I kept for long time was a little t-shirt that said "Jesus loves me" on it. It reminded me of the day Joe wore it to a picnic. I showed him off that day. There were other "snowflakes" there with special needs and I was feeling very blessed. I am repetitive with saying Joey was special, but it is the truth.

Don't clone a snowflake!

There is a lost world looking for love. Everyone desires a love story. To walk in the fruit of God's spirit is the "ultimate" love story and every soul just needs to ask God and receive their own personal ultimate love story. God's reality is He gives and He gave me freedom from years of grief, freedom of any bitterness, and freedom of the nagging "whys." Especially the one of "why" does a son go to heaven before the parents do? God's grace is sufficient in hours of grief and love of Christ brings gratitude that life can go for the good of others, to bless and encourage others in similar circumstances. I have to repeat "God is a good God, a giver." God gave me strength and love in my grief in the reality of living without Joe. I mourned but I think the turning point was when I choose one day to stop mourning and just let Jesus heal my heart. I was blessed in my grieving as God comforted. God is ever near as a loving friend.

I would find myself talking to Joe when going through his stuff. Like, "Hey Joe, how do you feel about me giving your car seat to a baby who has a heart problem?" Then I would quote verses from bible like, "It's more blessed to give than receive, Joey."

I don't think I wanted to give up being mom to Joe. I believe I don't have to either.

Desiree loved that car seat and she didn't want to give it up but was too big for it. It was given to the baby with heart issues. After it disappeared, Desiree noticed, yelling, "Where's my chair?" She soon learned to live without it, but not without stomping her feet.

I had a divine appointment with the mother of "heart" baby. I offered her hope. We developed a friendship and gave encouragement to one another. *Trusting the Lord was our* **hope**.

Even when all looks hopeless we need to trust in God. One day I was thinking to myself what and how does one really trust? I happened to have some repair work in my clothes closet when I wondering if I really knew what trust meant. As I nailed a small piece of wood to fix this certain spot I noticed it was going in wrong. The wood was going in slanted instead of straight. I thought, Oh just trust God to help, and I just lined it up as straight as I could so I wouldn't have to start over. I was amazed at how it fit in perfectly. I had no carpentry skills. I think it was a little lesson on "trust" in my closet. Things work out better in the end despite a bad start when trusting God. I just had to not force change but trust that God is doing it even when I can't see it right away. To put it another way, I believe trust is believing God's promises when we don't know the answers and just exercising faith that God does what he does the best, heals and restores.

"God is always faithful as the scripture Lamentations 3; 23 says, 'Great is His faithfulness; his loving kindness begins afresh each day," (The Living Bible). God was faithful in the everyday stuff.

A year after Joe's passing we were out for a drive (Desiree was four-and-a-half years) and we drove by the hospital. Desiree blurted out, "We should go to the hospital and see Joey and all the toys there." Obviously Desiree was too young to grasp the idea of death and time and thought that Joey lived in the hospital. I attempted to explain that Joey was no longer at hospital but in his new home in heaven and we would see him again when it was our turn to die. It was the wrong explanation as she replied with her own four-year-old understanding, "I want my turn." I ran out of explanations. We all missed Joey for a long time and Desiree and Joey were very close in age, so for her to miss him was a given. To counsel a four-year-old one needs Godly wisdom.

We had a, awesome, beautiful funeral to celebrate Joe's life.

Grandma, Darren, Desiree
(The day of Joe's funeral also Darren's ninth birthday.)

Chapter 12
Death and Children

HOW DOES ONE TALK ABOUT subjects like a death, pain, burying a child or a loved one? There is no one formula. Death of a child is not a pleasant conversation let alone actually living through the experience.

It's painstaking to hear a strange voice say, "Eighty dollars for plane fare and your son's body will be sent home for his funeral."

That's it? I thought. Wow are these just some parcels that are ready for shipping or are they actually meaning my son?

To the stranger on the phone line it was business as usual. With the grace of God I sputtered out a "thank you."

So I ask myself, "What's God view?" God sees it all and hears it all. I need to enter His room with a view so I can once again be filled with His peace. Seeing God's view, even just a glimpse, calms the voices that say your son is coming home in a box.

The following hymn says it better than me.

> Be still my soul
> (Author Katharina Amalia Dorothea von Schlegel)
>
> Bear patiently the cross of grief or pain
> Leave to thy God to order or provide
> In every change he faithful remains.
> Be still my soul, thy best heavenly friend is there
> Through the thorny ways and leads to a joyful end.
> Be still my soul, the hour is hastening on when
> We shall be together forever with the Lord,
> When disappointed, grief, and fear are gone,
> Sorrow forgotten, love purest joys restored.
> Be still my soul, when fears are past,
> safe and blessed.
> We shall meet at last.

God's holy presence in the waiting room of intensive care at Children's Hospital is the same presence as when a phone call says, "A box with your son is on its way." It is the same presence that was in the waiting room where I heard the doctor say, "Your baby died."

The almighty presence says "peace be still," with a glorious hug that holds me close.

In my reflecting I am very thankful for all God provided. Joey's heart specialist was a caring doctor. His head seemed to have a heart connection and gave out hugs.

I'm thankful for Jesus. Seeing Joey in critical condition and being told that "my baby is dying" is a moment I cry "Jesus." In silent peace I knew Jesus was holding Joey and that was stronger than my pain.

It is sad to look around in a waiting room to see parents, doctors, and nurses with tears in their eyes.

What and how did my life come to this place and time? I felt my own heart ache for all the hurting parents. I still did not believe that I would also be in their places of heartache and grief within twenty-four hours. Jesus was so ever-present in that little waiting room. I glanced around wondering do they not know the Lord Jesus is here in this tiny room. None of us knew each other yet we were all there drawn together by heartaches, connected, by our dying children. I could only pray and I knew "God knows us all" even to the very number of our hairs on our head.

The compassionate doctor gently spoke the words none of us were prepared to hear. One young mother, who was so pretty yet so sad, was holding her baby who was her first child. She would be going home to no children and an empty room of baby furniture. My tears and heart cried for her pain. What a trauma and all I could do was my never ending prayers. I was also very young and hurting for Joey. Only those who had experienced of the loss of a child will truly know what I am talking about.

A Bible story talks about Shadrach, Meshach, and Abednego, who were thrown into a fiery furnace (Dan. 3:21–30). The three came out of the furnace without any burns at all. The Lord delivered them. When parents and families lose a child they also go into a furnace that has a name, grief. It's good to mourn but to come out of it possible, just like the three fellows in the story about the furnace. (Jesus was with them). Mathew 19:26 says, "Jesus looked at them and said 'With man this is impossible, but with God all things are possible.'"

A waiting room is a "hot seat" or furnace for those hoping their child survived a surgery, an accident, or even birth. Tears and prayers entered the waiting room at the hospital as we waited to hear a doctor's report.

I cried out, "God is here" in the tiny room, only to hear a doctor respond, "Are you okay?" I replied, "Yes, do you know where I am coming from?" And he nodded with a "Yes, I know, I know." We both knew I was talking about my faith in a good God. I silently said to myself, "Thank you, God, for a kind doctor!"

I wanted to talk in that waiting room but grief and tears were too loud. I continued my prayers in silence. Finally, I had an opening to speak with the young mother holding the baby that was dying in her arms. To my surprise she said she always prays, too, and reads her Bible. We were sisters in the Lord and the spirit of God brought us strangers together. We comforted each other with just "knowing" that we understood. We didn't need to share words out loud, our heart aches spoke volumes. God's love was great in that waiting room, giving strength in our grief. We had a fiery furnace to go through called heart break. We felt pain but knew our babies were being held in God's hands. God's word is real and we did not fear death.

How many waiting rooms in the world must hold such dreaded times when children leave their parents too soon. God takes our pain as our focus is on Him. I do not want to waste my sorrow but instead share God's love, the love that has no end.

Bereavement is another tough word co-existing with words like grief, death, and pain. No matter what term the words mean sorrow and only God has all the answers.

The Bible says "we all have a time to be born and a time to die" yet does an accident mean it was their time? I don't know, but the word of God is true, which says we all have a free will. And if someone chooses to drink and drive there are terrible consequences. God does not make us puppets and choices determine much of what happens. Many innocent lives are lost tragically which could have been prevented.

Prayer covers and protects us in our choices. The Bible says "we have not because we have not asked." I am thankful for the covering of prayers of the saints. In Christ we have to be still and listen to God's voice.

If one decides to jump off a cliff they are naturally not in God's will. God allows us to choose. I heard it said that if God created a world with no problems we would lose the free agency to choose. In the beginning in the Garden of Eden there were no problems until free choice made a bad choice. Adam listened to Satan and fell into sin, disobeying God to not eat of one tree and mankind has been paying for it ever since. That tells me choices need to be taken seriously, as per the Bible: "Choose this day who you will serve" (Josh. 24:15).

A time to be born and a time to die is a part of life. To rise above life's difficulties and traumas one needs God's wisdom; trusting God *in* all things not necessarily *for* all things. Prayer and God's word will build, helping one become more and more Christ-like. As one looks into the face of Jesus, all the things of this world become increasing dim, giving hope for a future. *Hope is from God* and He *is the hope for the world.*

In the initial days of grieving my son's loss, I could not sit and just miss him so I began to write and fill my days. I wrote letters to my absent child. For me, it helped me walk through my pain and heartache. Walking through the door of sorrow is possible. I like to include the letters below, as this book is Joey's story, my "*snowflake.*"

Letter #1

Dear Joey

Hi, its mom. It's been awhile since we talked. Sometimes it's too painful trying to live without you. I'll have to live on and "accept the things I cannot change, change the things I can, and the wisdom to know the difference." I believe I have now accepted the fact you are not in my home here on earth but in your new home in heaven. I am sure it is very beautiful.

Yesterday I had quite a day, Joey. I went to a meeting for moms of Down syndrome children. The same one as me and you used to go to together. Felt very strange to go without you. I went anyway because I sensed a special bond to the mothers. It's because of you I know them a bit and it was nice to visit them. I think of them as "special moms." I think it bothered me as I was constantly thinking about you. The little boys Clint and Dennis were there and I couldn't help but remember how they hovered over you. Clint was very affectionate, giving your mom lots of kisses and many hugs. He even took my hand and took me on a walkabout. Joey, he can walk now and seemed like he wanted to show off. Joey, he is only five months older then you. I must say I sure enjoyed visiting Clint more than anyone at the meeting. Am sure you would have too, maybe the two of you would have grown into friends forever. Do you remember Dennis? He was a bit of a clown and we all loved hearing him sing out on van rides "Old MacDonald Farm." The children sure are getting big and Down syndrome did not seem to be on my mind, even though that is what brought us all together. All I thought about was "Jesus and you." The company was special Joey, but there was strangeness, an absence felt because you weren't with me. I am trying to live in the now, knowing you are just over yonder waiting for me but I will always miss you.

I didn't know, Joey, what people were talking about when they said the "firsts," the firsts of special times after losing a loved one until yesterday. It was the first time your momma was around Down syndrome children since you left. The first Christmas with you being gone was very difficult Joey. Yet it was so close after your funeral, twenty-five days to be exact, I think I was pretty sad on the inside, numbness. But now I let my feelings out. Yesterday at the meeting was one of those times when I felt strong feelings. They were all little boys there with Down syndrome. I so secretly was wishing one of them would magically become you. (As always Jesus helped with His love.) Joey, I know I am in His hands the same as you are. When I read my Bible, I find strength from Jesus. I just read that, "Faith restores the spirit. When one has faith nothing will crush him, not even death. For faith gives one insight that there is no death in the spirit; because Jesus lives, you shall also live."

Praise God Joey, we live in Jesus. I love you. Momma

P.S. Joey, I showed off your picture to everyone at the meeting and I still have it where I can see it every day.

Letter #2

November 22, 1983

Dear Joey

Today is your sister's birthday. Desiree is four years old already. Wish you were here to help celebrate. I know you are a party lover at heart. Today you are in my thoughts as it's also only three days away from your memorial day, November 25th. I am thinking about this time last year when you were in the hospital for that last surgery, your heart surgery.

Today I was searching through some drawers to find Desiree's mittens as it is snowing for Desiree's birthday. As I was hunting for gloves I found your little yellow bunting bag way back in the closet. I decided to give it to Desiree for her dolls. I went on looking for more winter clothes and found in my old dresser your favorite things stored away. Joe, I found your favorite squeaky orange doggie. I think it was my favorite too as it was so much fun to watch you play it and your Donald duck. Your clown and the favorite t-shirt from the hospital were all safely tucked away in the drawer. Your fuzzy new shoes were in there too, the ones that were bought for your trip home from hospital. You never got to wear them. Boy, everything in that drawer brought back special memories. I could imagine you watching as I pondered over your things. It was another one of my peaceful moments, sensing Jesus presence. I sure love you, Joey, and I think even more as time passes if that's possible. Your momma is not looking forward to November 25th. I'm assured Jesus is with me even if I am by myself on that Memorial Day. Joey, you would have been two-and-a-half years old when your sister turns four years old. In my mind I picture how much you would have grown, how much bigger you would have been and I know you would be more handsome and beautiful. Anyways, as I write this to you today you fill up my mind with peaceful thoughts. I'm off to do a birthday party Joey. I made her Winnie the Pooh cake, not that perfect but Desiree loves it. I asked your sister if I could take a picture of her with her cake and as I snapped the picture she yelled out, "Smile, Winnie, say cheese." It made me laugh. I have sad thoughts of you not being here but I can still laugh out loud. We miss you Joey, and love you always.

Love mom

Letter #3

Dear Joey

Been awhile since I wrote you a letter, yet you stay on my mind. Today I was visiting a friend of ours, Dennis and his mom. Remember Joe the time Dennis hugged you so tight we had to pull him off you. I seem to have a special love come over me whenever I am around those with Down syndrome. Dennis's mom brought along some pictures. Dennis had a glow even in the pictures. I had to smile and think about how society often thinks that it is sad to have a Down syndrome baby yet I believe parents are blessed in such a special way. I was Joey.

Dennis loves wrestling now and has memorized the time that it comes on TV. I thought that was so encouraging to see how he enjoys special things. I have to wonder what your special interests would have been. Maybe I'll know one day. For now, I love and miss you.

Love mom

Letter #4

Dear Joseph

I still have that feeling sometimes that you are close by. Of course right now I have a reason as tomorrow would have been your birthday, that special day I will always remember and think about you. This past year has brought me some pretty special friends, Joey. One of these friends wrote me a letter, filled with encouraging words and support as she knew it was your birthday and I was missing you. I felt so reassured again about how your little life was not in vain. The letter came in a beautiful card and two beautiful yellow roses. Little did my friend know that yellow roses will forever remind me of you. I think she's another handmaiden of the Lord. I really miss you today Joey.

God is ever present and I feel its okay to just cry. Sometimes there's a wound that flares up in my heart. I have to wonder if your health would have been okay to have a birthday party tomorrow. Funny things moms think. Surely it would have been the best ever as all the surgeries were done and over with.

It's been quite a week Joe. Last night I attended a ladies group I go to where we all take turns sharing stories. I was able to share your story Joey. God showed me how you are still showing love through your story. One lady came and told me that she has learned to love a baby named Joey who she has never met. That made me cry but tears of joy with the presence of Gods Holy Spirit, the comforter. But Joey the tears felt like healing tears. I was kind of wondering foolishly if God still loved me because He had you instead of me. Thank God for His Love as it brings me gratitude that I know I won't park or stay in a place of grieving. My letters to you are like stepping stones to walk through loosing you.

Guess what, today I went out and bought two roses. I'm not sure if they were for you or me, as you would have been two years old and it was your first birthday away. I bought one yellow rose with you in mind and a red one for your love. Today I went by myself and laid the yellow one on your grave site. Tomorrow on your birthday I'll take the red one to your grave site. It was a very short drive. I had to stop for a red light and in my view was the cemetery. Alone in my car and thoughts I silently murmured, "That's where I laid my son's body, but just his body." As I began feeling very alone with my sadness, the song "Amazing Grace" came on the radio with only bag pipers playing. I started to hum along thinking, "what timing," just another natural supernatural reminder that I was not alone. How awesome Joey that the God that is with you is with me. I wished the short ride to your grave site had been longer as God was there. I will remember your birthday always. "Amazing Grace" along with yellow roses is in my heart and memory of my Joseph. I talked to you at your grave Joey. Did you hear me? I know, you are in heaven but I couldn't help myself just in case you were listening as Jesus was so ever present. I know also you are happy and missing you or not, I'm happy for you. There's a candle burning in my heart for you, Joey.

Happy Birthday! I miss and love you. Mom

Letter #5

Dear Joey

Guess what! Darren and Desiree attended Bible school this week. Desiree could hardly wait to get there but Darren wasn't as excited. On the last day Darren only wanted to pick up his crafts and leave. I had to talk to that brother of yours and encourage him to stay. I even reminded him Jesus was there and maybe you.

You would have been proud to hear him read his part in a play about "fishers of men." Darren spoke clearly and well and then sang cheerfully along with his classmates. It was beautiful to hear all the children singing about Jesus. You must hear a lot of beautiful singing but Mom wished you had been there anyway. I get a little sad when I am around children still as I start to miss you. I am blessed knowing you are happy in your new home. The Lord does give "beauty for ashes."

Love mom

Letter #6

Hi Joe: It's mom again. You're on my mind today. I had a phone call from my neighbor, Ann. She said, "Can Joey and I come over?" It took me by surprise as I didn't know she named her new baby "Joey." Well Joey, she came over for a visit as she wanted to offer condolences about me losing you. Ann said she totally forgot about you when she named her baby. I think she felt a little bad about it all. I assured her it was all fine and that I was happy she likes the good name of "Joey." Sometimes I think some people are sadder than I am. I guess they don't understand how God is my grace and strength. It was an interesting day, Joe.

Miss you. Love Momma

P.S. I have a poem for you Joey that I jotted down on Memorial Day because I love and miss you.

You entered my heart one summer day,
in such a special way.
My heart broke one autumn day, in such a
tearful way,
when you left for a new home in heaven.
How do I thank you for giving me such love
and leaving it behind when you left?

My heart overflows,
You are my sunshine, no matter summer, autumn
or winter.
My special snowflake all year long!
Love mom on this Memorial Day

Today autumn is in the air. I take a walk and wonder, what Joey would say about this beautiful day? I think I know. Joey would say, "It's beautiful, Mom." My mind wanders and I recall a conversation with some old friends. They told me they lighted a candle when Joey was in hospital for that last time and said that candle burned a week after the wick was done. That thought warmed my heart as I walked along.

We know that in the Bible after Jesus died many of His friends remembered and talked among themselves about Jesus the Savior of the world. I'm sure when the disciples of the Lord walked miles the memory stayed with them. In prison and beaten they had memories that were close to their hearts. There really is something to be said about the last time spent with someone precious. Below is a story about a special memory.

"I Remember"

They had gathered for the evening meal as they always did. The long bare table looked as uninviting as did the simple meal of coarse bread and a cup of water. The men sat at the table dejectedly, some of them mere shells of what they had once been. At various points around the room the guards stood as figures of authority that constantly threatened the life of anyone who dared oppose it. There was no God there, unless it was the unseen power that controlled the guards or so it seemed.

One of the men sitting at the table was holding his chunk of bread in his hand. He was thinking back to the little church he had led in his hometown an eternity ago. The bread had been a symbol of something that bound people together. Here it had come to mean something else: something oppressive in place.

Yet slowly, deliberately, the man tore a piece of his bread and laid it on his plate. Quietly he said, as if to himself, "I remember" and ate the bread.

A few of the other men at the table had noticed what he had done. To some of them, images out of a dim and distant past floated up like ghosts from the recesses of their minds. Memories that had almost been wiped out by the daily horror they now lived in. Some of them, embolden by the actions of the first, likewise took a piece of bread and slowly ate it one by one so as not to attract attention. As they did so their eyes met the eyes of others as if to say by their glances, "I too, remember." The leader then nodding almost imperceptibly took his tin cup of water and murmured, "I remember" and drank. The men around him again followed suit.

So quietly had the exchange taken place that none of the guards and indeed many of those sitting at the table did not realize the significance of what had just taken place. But for the participants, warmth unlike anything that they had felt in a long time was burning in their breasts. They felt somehow strengthened and charged by the experience.

(Author unknown)

Today is Remembrance Day on the calendar for those many who lost their lives in the war. Everyone has remembrances of their own. They are marked down in one's heart and soul. Memories are part of the invisible where changes occur in one's attitude for both character and values. Even in the realm of memories we choose to capture the good and delete the unnecessary. Many can be a warm blanket to bring comfort and some as a reminder to be thankful. Those who suffered in war and prisons, I'm sure, found comfort in God who gives hope for a better future. It is a beautiful, significant thing to remember and be remembered.

Chapter 13
Goodbyes

MY CALENDAR TOLD ME THAT tomorrow was exactly one month to the date since Joey left for his new home. Remembering was normal when I missed Joe. I silently whispered, "I feel like coming home today to see you, Joey."

Instead I went about doing my normal daily routine, enjoying a coffee, sending Darren out to do his newspaper route as I watched Desiree playing. Everything seemed momentarily normal except it was Christmas Eve and Joey's first Christmas without us.

I missed my snowflake!

It was a process to accept that Joe said goodbye.

The last trip to hospital, Joey wore a beautiful royal blue outfit, dressed like royalty that he was. I ended up choosing this same outfit for his burial clothes, as it brought out the color of his beautiful blue eyes. Joe touched many lives with the glow of his beautiful blue eyes, the ones that sparkled with the love of Jesus.

I recall one special goodbye when the grandparents met me and Joey at the airport to drive us to the hospital. They were so happy to see Joey. Joey stole the show, happy, alert and giggling. After Joey was done showing off he took a deep breath and gave his grandparents his contagious smile. I called it Joe's farewell goodbye smile to his grandparents. To describe it is almost impossible. In the moment we sensed this could be our goodbye to Joe. It was that still, small voice that says, "Farewell my son." It was a defined premonition that you I just knew something was up.

Joe and I were inseparable on that last day before heart surgery.

Little did I know that day that it be only a week later and I would experience the greatest sorrow of my life. I found it strange how Joe was so clingy that awesome last day. Joe just wanted to play, flirting with the hospital staff and flashing them his contagious smiles. Joe did show some contempt as those white jackets were associated with pain.

My touch always brought a settling down for Joe and Jesus settled me with His touch. For a baby that the doctors suggested I put in an institution Joe had a strong heart. Physically it was his heart that took his life yet his heart of determination kept him alive and fighting right up to the very day he left my side. Joey fought the effects of open heart surgery for seven days until his little body finally grew too weak.

I remain thankful for the "closeness" with Joey, my baby boy.

The dreams I had prior to this day, which all pointed to a big goodbye, were put in the back of my mind. One of the dreams was a vision about flowers. I saw flowers in my living room and these same flowers at a funeral room. After this dream I knew a funeral was imminent. I never believed that it might be Joe. I now know God was speaking in the quietness of the night.

I remember driving passed this funeral home one day and thinking I dreamed I was in there. In the dream I saw people I knew, what clothes they wore and what I said, which was, "I wish people could think about God everyday instead of waiting for a funeral." I remembered all the details.

I even had a dream, whereby, I saw Joey in a little white casket, the flowers on it, and the cross pendent on his blue outfit, which of course came to pass, down to every detail . I cannot understand how I didn't get it, Joe's goodbye and celebration of his life was just around the corner.

As a mother totally in love with my child I believed I was just anxious of the pending surgery. Joey was my pride and joy. I did not worship Joe, I worship Jesus, but Jesus was with both Joey and I. Having idols or worship of people or things separate one from God. Joey helped me come into a closer relationship with God.

I had many other dreams, prophecies, visits, and forewarnings about Joe's passing away. Even my grieving happened in a dream. It was Joe's anniversary date November 25th, one year later that I had a dream about being in an elevator at the Children's Hospital with Joe's nurses, five in total count. We talked about me staying at the hospitable the previous summer. I began to tell them all about Joe's heart surgery and broke down weeping excessively. We hugged. They said they too loved Joey. The Holy Spirit comforted me in a dream that helped me with grief. I felt healing rise in the deep crevices of my heart. Isaiah 53:3 says, "He was despised and rejected and forsaken by men, a Man of sorrows and pains, and acquainted with grief." "God knows well what grief is and it is by his stripes we are healed (Isaiah 53:5).

I needed the great physician "Jesus." Jeremiah 30:17: "For I will bring health to your bones and I will heal your wounds."

The Bible is full of references to God's healing.

Isaiah 30:18: "Blessed are those who wait for Him to help them." It was a year to the date that I had a healing dream. Waiting upon God what else could I do? I know we can all "bank on" God's word. God knew my wound I had from losing Joey and was my healer. Even in pain I had experienced a good God and His love.

Joe's story is all about God's goodness and how he will bring good out of all things. The roots of my character and faith in God went deeper. I believe the whole purpose of life is to grow in *God's love.*

One little *snowflake* named *Joe* made a *difference* in this mother's journey.

God's glory shines through in weaknesses and human limitations. 11 Corinthians 12:9 clearly tells me the strength of God will rest and cover our weaknesses, therefore experiences of both joy and suffering is in the end all about Jesus.

Christians can thrive in the midst of sufferings because of Jesus. I can choose to be a Christian consumer only desiring blessings or decide to grow when sufferings happen in this world.

Sometimes we fail to see that the choice is ours to heal. We can choose to stay where pain lives or to grow and thrive. Memories stay embedded but they can melt or freeze. Philippians 3:13 tells us we do have a part to play, as it tells us to forget those things that are behind "determined" to move on. God would not tell us to do something that He would not help us with.

Jesus endured the cross yet he rose again and His pain and sorrow was not wasted. Jesus chose the cross so that we may be saved. I believe one should not waste their sorrow but follow Jesus' example. Choose to allow God to do the inner healing while reaching out to help others.

Proverbs 3:5–6 will tells us what we should do:" Lean on, trust in and be confident in the Lord with all your heart and mind and do not rely on your own insight or understanding, in all your ways recognize and acknowledge Him and make plain and straight your paths".

Joe's story is a confirmation of God's faithfulness, His promises, His power and His presence.

As we come through to the other side of life's challenges we will develop perseverance and live as over-comers and become champions. Champions will tell you without a doubt that determination and persevering is necessary to win. The Bible tells us in the end who wins. Jesus is the champion of champions!

How awesome that a simple snowflake could teach so much about love. Joseph was sent from heaven to show me love and I caught on at first glance.

How can I conclude a book about love and sorrow?

I believe it would be *to give hope*, comfort, and a *message about love*.

God has a plan and purpose to everything under heaven. Psalm 139:13 says, "You knit me together in my mother's womb."

Joseph was not a mistake!

Don't Clone a Snowflake!

I am looking forward to the day king Jesus returns. There will be no more pain, no more suffering, no more death or funerals, no more tears, no more prejudiced and the children shall run and be free. I will not be surprised that His return will be before I face death. What a glorious day and a time to rejoice like never before as families and loved ones are reunited for eternity.

In the waiting room called "life" it would be better if we draw close to God before any sickness or suffering comes our way. God's will is to give us abundant life. 3 John 1:2 says, "Beloved I wish you all to prosper and be in health even as thy soul prospers." So sickness is not of God, nor accidents or traumas. Even birth defects are healed by God. The Bible says, "My people perish for lack of knowledge." We need to draw close to God.

God has a plan and a purpose to everything under heaven.

Joey's short life also had purpose. I enlisted in God's university called Love and I believe it's a major course in what God has for me to do in all-eternity.

Today is Josephs Memorial Day as I conclude his story.

This awesome baby boy has a story!

Joey's heart was golden (pure) and the fingerprint on my heart still shines. Thank you Joe, I love you so much forever.

A golden boy with a golden fingerprint!

Thanks to my good Father, the One who knows what one little snowflake can accomplish in a short time!

To everyone with trauma of any kind I would say *trust God*. It is a privilege to trust God so forget the "whys" and never give up on God. Even when I trusted God to heal I lost a baby but I know God brought me through. God enabled me to stand firmly with more compassion for those in similar circumstances. It takes a faithful God to help reach a place whereby I can now choose to give comfort more then to be comforted.

Stand on the word of God. Nahum 1:7 reads, "The Lord is good. A strength and stronghold in the day of trouble; He knows (recognizes, has knowledge of, and understands) those who take refuge and trust in Him." To come into God's perfect will instead of selfish seeking is to walk in God's goodness.

If I had a chance I would relive Joe's story. Unfortunately, life does not come with "Can I redo?" We only get one chance. It is wise to understand how short life really is.

In my amplified Bible, Proverbs 3:13–14 says "Happy (blessed, fortunate, and enviable) is the man who finds skillful and godly Wisdom, and the man who gets understanding (drawing it forth from God's word and life's experiences). For the gaining of it is better than the gaining of silver, and the profit of it is better than fine gold."

Joe's story is a life experience that I'm glad I didn't miss even if I cannot redo or relive it. It was a life changing, defining chapter of my life. The Lord prepared me for it and He took me through it. I will not understand it completely but I better understand God's love. God's healing is continual as He is a continual for all eternity. God's desire is healing for all and may happen in heaven.

I have an article dated 1981 and it brought joyful tears as I remember the closeness once again that I had with my baby boy, Joey. It's a goodbye letter from a grieving mom. Anyone who lost a child and trusts God will relate.

Dear Little Baby,

It's only three days since I lost you, and all I can do is cry. My grief at times seems unbearable. You were truly a miracle to me. We had wanted a baby for so long. There had been seven years of doctors and tests and finally I got pregnant, I knew it right away— within two weeks—and I was right. You were the answer to so many prayers. I didn't think anything would happen to you.

I'd have joyful thoughts of you and what our lives would be like together. I never felt so close to God, and each day I would thank Him for you and pray that I would have a healthy pregnancy.

Carrying you was the happiest time of my life. I love your father and to know that he and I and God had created human life together made me very happy every moment of the day.

But then I lost you . . . And when it happened, people felt our sadness—and even strangers felt our grief. A nurse hugged me. A lady at church cried with me and told me of the two babies she had lost. She told me how it still hurts her and how she knows I will never forget you. Friends prayed. Now you are with God in heaven—and can never really be taken from me—you are part of me.

I look at life differently with more compassion for others. Every moment is more precious.

I pray for another baby—but I know I will never have exactly the same feelings as I had with you.

I do not understand. I am not angry with God. I love Him and I know that He loves me, and you

were a beautiful gift from Him. I thank Him with all
my heart for our brief time together.

Love you. Mom

As mothers we both had hopes and dreams for our babies and
never believed anything would happen to our babies and never felt
so close to God. We had much in common in that we felt love from
nurses and strangers. We came away with a new attitude toward
life and remained grateful to God. We both experienced the "just
knowing." The "just knowing" happens and I believe it is God's
way of revealing and preparing for His purposes in our lives.

The mother in the letter had her own precious little snowflake
that she lost yet still loved and trusted God. Who knows what one
little snowflake can do?

I am sure if that mom lost her baby today instead of 1981,
it would be the same story. Spiritual and emotional needs stay
the same.

I would like to include the following two articles. The first is
one is from 1981 and the second from 2016. It was accidentally
sent to me on Facebook. I suspect God intervened just to show
how some things haven't changed through the years. I'll let the
stories speak for themselves.

"Love in Action" (1981)

"What a sweet-natured little fellow," said the woman,
nodding at my four-year-old.

"What's his name?" She had sat down on my park
bench where I watched my son fill his toy dump
truck with pebbles.

"It's Billy and yes he is a special boy," I answered
gratefully. I wasn't used to having strangers say nice

things about my child. Often, people would act as if Billy was invisible. I always wanted to say, "Its okay, you can talk to him or me about him. Just don't shut him out of your world."

My companion took a needlepoint design out of a bag to work on it. "One of my sons is retarded. He's grown up now and has a part-time job."

"Really?" A dozen questions popped into my mind, but I was distracted by a group of six to nine-year-old boys. Their laughter stopped when they saw Billy.

"What a weirdo," blurted one boy.

How I ached every time I heard that kind of remark! Out of the corner of my eye, I saw one of the boys mocking Billy's awkward walk. I thought: How dare you make fun of him—you with your strong bodies and minds?

I yearned for a bridge between them and my often rejected little boy. Oh Jesus, help me to speak lovingly, the way you would. Just then I heard calm, compelling voice from the other end of the bench. "Boys," said the woman, smiling at them. "You're right that Billy can't run or think as fast as you. But do you know what he can do."

The boys stopped and stared at her, wondering what she would say about this strange little fellow.

"Billy can watch you play and be your friend. Would you like to show him how you play?"

One by one, they lifted their eyebrows; they had reached a unanimous decision.

"Sure why not?" They started to move onto the play equipment—except for the boy who had imitated Billy.

"Hey Billy, want me to give you a ride on the turnabout?"

Billy looked my way, his expression showing that he knew something special had happened, I nodded, blinking back tears.

Thank You, gracious Jesus.

The loving woman beside me said, "God bless you."

The next article below is from over thirty years later. Education hasn't been enough to bring full acceptance of those with special needs. Society still has problems accepting those with disabilities.

From Facebook (2016):

If your kids are not around special need kids at school and have never been taught that not everyone is the same, you could take time to explain that to them because even though they may not be around these kids at school they will encounter them in their lives. Recently a child with autism was excluded from participating in a school trip and a child with Down syndrome was kicked out of a dance class because she couldn't keep up. There are children that nobody invites to parties, there are special kids who want to belong to a team but don't get selected because it's more important to win than include these children. Children with special needs are not so strange; they only want what everyone else wants; to be accepted. This is for all those wonderful children out there.

(Author unknown)

It is obviously a struggle sometimes for parents to mingle their special needs children into society. To see all children as unique is an attitude. May Jesus help us to appreciate our differences and love one another as He has first loved us.

God's way is to love one another and God's word should have the last say in this world of differences. Isaiah 44:6 says, "I am the first and the last: there is no other God."

There is good in this world despite the challenges life brings. Psalm 24:1 says, "The earth is the Lord's and the fullness thereof."

The other day it came to my attention that a well-known children's department store is having a beautiful Down syndrome toddler on the front of their advertisement. Many special needs individuals are making their mark in this world and taking their rightful place in society and they deserve a big shout of amen, as how many others can say the same?

Don't Clone a snowflake!

The following article reminds me to be careful in labeling and what we say and think about individuals. L (By Edgar A. Guest)

I'd rather see a sermon than hear one any day.
I'd rather one should walk with me than merely
point the way.
The eye's a better pupil than the ear,
Fine counsel is confusing,
But example's is always clear;
And the the best of all preachers
Are the men who live their creeds,
For to see good put in action
Is what everybody needs.
I soon can learn to do it
If you'll let me see it done;
I can watch your hands in action,
But your tongue too fast may run,

And the lecture you deliver
May be very wise and true,
But I'd rather get my lessons
By observing what you do;
For I might misunderstand you
And the high advice you give,
But there's no misunderstanding
How you act and live.

That being said I am sure that Down syndrome toddler on a clothing advertisement photo said volumes with his smile and arms held out. The photo said it all.

Our life is a journey and in the mist of sorrow there is growth. The following is a poem about sorrow.

I walked a mile with pleasure
She chatted all the way
But I left none the wiser
With all she had to say
I walked a mile with sorrow
And never a word said she
But oh, the things I learned with her
When sorrow walked with me.

(Robert Browning Hamilton)

We all need to remove our colored glasses and become more loving and accepting. We're all unique like snowflakes.

"**Don't** Clone a Snowflake"

I must reaffirm that it was for me in my darkest hour, that I got to know the great "faithful, loving, God" and the sound of Amazing Grace.

Thanks for making such a difference in my life.

Thanks for teaching me love.

To Joe ... "SEE YOU SOON." See you at the biggest party ever when we meet. By the way, every snowflake is invited!

I pray my readers came to know Joey through his story as a little beautiful person who everybody loved, especially me.

I think it is appropriate to conclude by acknowledging the positively great work of the pioneers and educators who have laid so much groundwork, working with integration of handicapped in normal schools. May God bless all who continue to support and love those with special needs. With God's grace and love we can move mountains.

God loves us equally yet differently. May we move forward in His complete love. Jude 21 (AMP): "Guard and keep yourselves in the LOVE of GOD; expect and patiently wait for the mercy of our Lords Jesus Christ (the Messiah)—which will bring you into eternal life."

I can't wait to see you Joe. Thanks for the honor of being my gift and son from our Heavenly Father. Thank you, Jesus!

I hear the music playing in the background; it is the song "Amazing Grace; as I end this story. Awe, just another of God's friendly reminders. He's watching over me and you. God bless us all!

See you soon Joe!!!

I will always remember!!!

Printed in Canada